HELEN WILLIAMS

The Ultimate Destination Guide for Eugene and Springfield 2nd Edition

From Ducks to Vineyards: An Insider's Tour of Eugene-Springfield's Must-Visit Places and Unique Experiences

This book is dedicated to my family, whose love and encouragement have been my beacon. Your support has transformed my dream into reality, and for that, my gratitude knows no bounds.
Whether you seek the thrill of the forests, the peace of the waters, or the vibrancy of local culture, may this book enrich your journey and leave you with lasting memories.
Let us embark on this exploration together, united by the thrill of discovery.

Welcome to Eugene-Springfield

Contents

1

Your Gateway to Adventure in Eugene-Springfield

Welcome to an exhilarating journey through the vibrant heart of Oregon in

"The Ultimate Destination Guide for Eugene-Springfield."

This book is more than just a guide; it's a portal to the soul of a region I have the privilege of calling home. Whether you're a curious traveler or a proud local, these pages promise to unveil the magic and wonders of Eugene and Springfield in ways you've never imagined.

Imagine a place where every turn is a new story, every path leads to an undiscovered treasure. That's what awaits you here. This guide is your key to unlocking the rich tapestry of experiences, from the adrenaline rush of a Duck game at Autzen Stadium to the hypnotic rhythms of a concert at the Cuthbert Amphitheater. Here, time is a canvas for joy, and every moment is ripe with potential.

This treasure trove of a guide is thoughtfully curated to cater to all – whether you're a lively toddler or a spirited centenarian. Dive into our insider's look at the most breathtaking hiking trails, indulge in the refined tastes of top-tier wineries, unleash creativity with unique crafts, and bask in a diverse range of arts and entertainment. Nature lovers, too, will find their haven in the best spots for immersing in nature and wildlife.

Whether you find solace in the gentle flow of the river, with boats and kayaks painting a serene picture, or seek the thrill of mountain biking across picturesque landscapes, this guide will lead you there.

But, before we embark, let me share some personal insights from my 25-year love affair with this region, insights that are as real as they are endearing. The idiosyncrasies of Eugene's streets, a quirky testament to its unique character, and the smart hacks for navigating parking (yes, those meter readers are vigilant!) are part of the charm that I've come to adore.

Since my arrival in the fall of 2000, Eugene has captivated me with its pulsating energy, its artistic flair, and its unabashed love for life – rain or shine. My first encounter during the Civil War week of football frenzy was an eye-opener to the community spirit that throbs in this University town.

Eugene's narrative is rich and varied – from being the only university with a Disney character as a mascot to being the birthplace of a global sportswear giant. It's a city where history intertwines with contemporary culture, where education and athletics have forged legends.

So, come with me. Let's wander the river paths, immerse in the eclectic, and discover why, in every sense, Eugene is not just a place, but a feeling. Prepare to fall in love, just as I did, with a city that forever echoes in your heart as home. Welcome to Eugene-Springfield, where every day is an invitation to explore and celebrate.

2

Arriving in Eugene Welcome to the World's Coziest Airport!

Eugene Airport (EUG) – A Little Hub of Surprises

I love flying in and out of Eugene Airport! It is large enough to have many of the major airlines, such as:

1. American
2. United
3. Avelo
4. Southwest
5. Allegiant
6. American Southwest
7. Delta
8. Alaska

But it is small enough to check in and get to the terminal without breaking a sweat.

If you get a chance, grab a bite at the restaurant on the main floor. They are quick and the food is good.

We take our Oregon Ducks very seriously in Eugene.

You can see these unique Ducks throughout Eugene.

Transportation – Your Adventure Begins Here!

Options for getting to downtown Eugene which is only about 10 miles to the heart of Eugene.

Renting a car: The car rental booths are located on the main floor next to the luggage terminal

Uber and Lyft are available on your mobile apps

Executive Taxi 541 228 7737

Oregon Taxi 541 434 8294

We also have Wheelchair and Disabled Taxi Services at 541 954 1950

Amtrak – The Vintage Way to Travel in Eugene

Amtrak offers a unique and historic mode of transportation in Eugene, providing a blend of nostalgic charm and modern convenience. The Eugene Amtrak station, located at 433 Willamette St, Eugene, OR 97401, is not just a transit point but a piece of history.

A Journey through Time:

1. **Historic Masonry Station** - Built in 1908 for the Southern Pacific Railroad, Eugene's Amtrak station is one of the remaining five masonry stations along the original Southern Pacific Railroad's west coastline. Its architecture speaks volumes of the early 20th-century railroad era.
2. **National Register of Historic Places** - The significance of the Eugene station transcends its functionality. Listed on the National Register of Historic Places on August 16, 2008, the station is a landmark that echoes the rich railroading past of the region.
3. **Central Location** - Situated in the heart of Eugene, the station is conveniently located within walking distance of some of the city's finest hotels and restaurants. This central location makes it an ideal starting point for exploring the city.
4. **Gateway to Exploration** - Using Amtrak from Eugene opens up a world of exploration along the Pacific coast and beyond. It's a journey that offers scenic views, comfort, and a slower pace of travel, allowing passengers to savor the experience.
5. **Modern Amenities** - Despite its historical significance, the station is equipped with modern amenities to ensure a comfortable experience for travelers. This includes waiting

areas, ticketing services, and customer assistance.

6. **Connection to Nature** - The train routes from Eugene showcase the stunning landscapes of Oregon, from lush forests to rugged coastlines, making the journey as memorable as the destination.

Traveling with Amtrak:

- **Contact Information:** For schedules, bookings, and inquiries, visit Amtrak.com or call (541) 683-7907.
- **Accessibility:** Amtrak ensures accessibility for all travelers, making it a convenient option for everyone.

Traveling by Amtrak from Eugene is more than just a mode of transportation; it's a journey that connects you with the history of rail travel and the beauty of the Pacific Northwest. Whether you're a history enthusiast, a leisure traveler, or a commuter, the Amtrak experience in Eugene offers a unique and enjoyable way to travel.

If you are driving- Eugene is located about 100 miles south of Portland, or 407 miles from the California-Oregon border on Hwy 5.

3

Exploring Transportation Options in Eugene

Bus Travel with LTD - For convenient city travel, the Lane Transit District (LTD) offers extensive bus routes. This network connects various parts of the city, making it a reliable and Eco-friendly choice for daily commutes or casual trips. Check out their website for times and places. https://www.ltd.org/route-schedules-maps/

Electric Bike Rentals at Pedego - For a more personalized and adventurous experience, consider renting an electric bike from Pedego Electric Bikes. They offer rentals ranging from 2 to 6 hours. Additionally, for those with young children, they provide Burley Trailers suitable for kids under 7. Pedego also organizes private bike tours along the scenic Willamette River. For more details or to make a reservation, you can email them at info@pedegoeugene.com or contact them at 541-650-0650. check out their website at https://pedegoelectricbikes.com/dealers/eugene/ for more information.

City's Blue Bike Program - The City of Eugene boasts an innovative bike-sharing program with over 40 stations featuring 350 distinctive blue bikes. This system allows residents and visitors to easily rent and return bikes across the city, facilitating short urban trips. To access these bikes, download the designated app or visit www.PeaceHealthRides.com for further information.

Yellow E-Scooters This pilot program that I hope will be around in the near and distant future. Here's how they work:

To start scooting, download the _Superpedestrian app_ and find an available scooter.

Once you've located one, make sure the throttle LED is green, indicating it's ready to be used. There is a QR code located on the top of the scooter's handlebars. Scan that code using the Superpedestrian app to unlock the scooter and wait up to 10 seconds for the throttle LED to turn white, indicating the scooter is unlocked and ready to use. After that, you're set to start riding.

Each scooter has an onboard geofence that can slow or stop a scooter in designated no-ride zones. These zones are highlighted on the app's map. Riders are encouraged to wear a helmet, use roads and cycle lanes, park safely, and only have one rider per scooter.

It costs $2 to unlock a scooter and is 39 cents a minute. If you park a scooter in a designated parking corral, you will get $1 back toward your next ride. For more information check out: https://www.eugene-or.gov/3851/Bike-Share

4

Why Eugene? - More Than Just Ducks and Hippies!

Eugene's Hidden Gems: A Treasure Trove of Attractions

Welcome to a chapter that promises to transform your view of Eugene. Forget about keeping secrets – this book is your all-access pass to the hidden wonders of this dynamic city. With each page, you'll unearth the lesser-known, yet equally mesmerizing facets of Eugene, taking you far beyond the common perceptions of just Ducks and hippies.

A Culinary Odyssey: Eugene's Gastronomic Landscape

Prepare to embark on a culinary adventure that will tantalize your taste buds and leave you craving more. Eugene, a city often underestimated in its culinary offerings, is a hidden Eden for food lovers. It's not just the quantity of restaurants we boast; it's the quality, diversity, and stories behind each establishment that make dining here an unforgettable experience.

The onslaught of COVID-19 battered many small businesses, but like Eugene's resilient spirit, our culinary scene has emerged more substantial and vibrant. Many of our beloved eateries have not only survived but have also reinvented themselves, offering new flavors and experiences and testament to the indomitable spirit of our local entrepreneurs.

In this chapter, we're not just listing restaurants. We invite you to join us through the aromas, flavors, and textures that define Eugene's culinary landscape. From quaint cafes hidden in plain sight to bustling eateries with stories as rich as their menus, each place you'll discover here adds a unique thread to the fabric of Eugene's gastronomic tapestry.

So, grab your fork (chopsticks or fingers) and dive into Eugene's culinary heart. Here, every meal is not just food; it's an exploration, an experience, and an adventure. Welcome to the city where every dish tells a story, and every bite is a memory in the making. Let's feast!

Cafe Yumm - They have several locations and can be delivered to your home or hotel. They specialize in vegetarian, vegan, and gluten-free special diets but also have chicken. It is very affordable and fresh. My personal favorite is the **Yumm! 'N' Greens**® served on a bed of organic field greens and crowned with tortilla chips.

5th Street Market, located at 296 E 5th Ave, Eugene, OR 97401, has a variety of delicious restaurants all in one centralized area. My personal favorite is **Cafe Glendi**. They make fresh spanakopita, which is always delicious. Check out their menu on their website: https://glendicafe.com/

Hideaway Bakery is nestled at 3377 E. Amazon Drive in Eugene, Oregon. Hideaway Bakery is more than just a bakery; it's a community cornerstone where the aroma of freshly baked sourdough, pastries, and wood-fired pizzas creates a warm, inviting atmosphere. Known for its artisanal offerings and unique flavors, the bakery showcases handcrafted goods made with locally sourced, organic ingredients. From their sourdough bread with its perfect crust to the delicate pastries and fresh kinds of pasta, each item reflects the skill and passion of their bakers. Hideaway Bakery stands out for its exceptional culinary delights and as a gathering place for the community. It offers a farm cart open daily and is a hub for locals and visitors to come together and enjoy life's simple pleasures. Call 541-868-1982 or visit them at https://hideawaybakery.com/

Black Wolf Supper Club, nestled in the heart of Eugene, Oregon, is a beacon of culinary innovation and social dining. This unique establishment redefines the dining experience with its fusion of exquisite flavors and a vibrant atmosphere, encapsulating the essence of a modern supper club. The menu, a masterpiece of culinary creativity, offers a diverse range of dishes, each crafted with the finest ingredients and an eye for detail. The club's ambiance, reminiscent of classic supper clubs with a contemporary twist, provides the perfect backdrop for a memorable evening. Whether it's for a casual dinner, a special occasion, or a night out with friends, Black Wolf Supper Club offers an unparalleled experience that combines the joys of fine dining with the warmth of community gathering, making it a must-visit destination in Eugene's thriving food scene. Call 541-687-8226 or visit https://www.blackwolfsupperclub.com for reservations.

Krob Krua is located at 1313 Pearl Street in Eugene, Oregon, and presents a unique and tantalizing culinary experience with its wood-fired Thai cuisine. This innovative restaurant offers a fresh take on traditional Thai dishes, infusing them with the distinctive flavors and aromas only wood-fired cooking can provide. The menu is a celebration of bold and authentic flavors, featuring dishes like Salmon Yellow Curry, Crispy Duck & Pineapple Red Curry, and Salt & Pepper Shrimp, each meticulously prepared to showcase the depth and complexity of Thai cuisine. The ambiance of Krob Krua combines a cozy, inviting atmosphere with a touch of modern elegance, making it a perfect destination for both casual lunches and intimate dinners. The fusion of classic Thai recipes with the unique twist of wood-fired cooking makes Krob Krua another must-visit for food enthusiasts seeking to explore new culinary horizons in Eugene's vibrant food scene. Call 541-636-6267 or visit https://www.krobkrua.com

When I started compiling my list, I realized that I could go on for pages and pages since Eugene and Springfield are filled with wonderful restaurants. I suggest you decide on what flavor and country your belly is desiring, then put it in your search engine to find a plethora of deliciousness waiting for your taste buds. Remember, keep it local; you can go to the chains anywhere.

5

Hikes and Bikes

Hikes: Trails with Tales

Spencer Butte is a popular hiking destination located in the south Eugene hills in Oregon, USA. It offers a challenging but rewarding hike with *stunning views* of the surrounding area.

The hike to the summit of Spencer Butte is approximately **2.5 miles round trip** and has an elevation gain of approximately 800 feet. The trail is well-maintained and easy to follow, but it can be steep in some areas and requires a moderate level of fitness.

Along the way, hikers will pass through a diverse landscape of oak savannas, Douglas fir forests, and rocky outcroppings. The summit of Spencer Butte offers breathtaking panoramic views of the Willamette Valley, the Cascade Range, and the city of Eugene.

I have hiked this several times. It has a great trail with benches along the way to rest. It is very popular and people bring their furry babies, so don't be surprised to meet a lot of animals. I recommend using walking poles if you have them, and use the bathrooms before you go up as there is nothing but trees and leaves if you need to go. Also, make sure you lock your car and do not leave anything that looks like it might make someone a nickel and a dime at the pawn store. Creepy thieves are everywhere, so be cautious.

Also, in the summer be careful of snakes and poison ivy.

Pisqua Arboretum and Trails 34901 Frank Parrish Road Eugene OR 97405 Whether you're looking for vigorous exercise, quiet contemplation, or a pleasant picnic, you will find it all here. You can come to enjoy the natural world while hiking the extensive network of trails or learn about local ecology with their nature walks and workshops. They celebrate mushrooms and wildflowers at our annual festivals. It doesn't matter if you are 2 or 102, it is a great way to enjoy the wonders of nature. I love hiking to the top and watching the sunset on the winter and summer solstice. It's almost magical.

I have been to several of their walks and hikes. I usually go with a friend, but meeting people who enjoy the same exercise and beauty adds another dimension to the experience.

Dorris Ranch Another little-known fact: Dorris Ranch is recognized as the first commercial filbert orchard in the United States and is listed on the National Register of Historic Places

Oregon's history with filberts started in 1892 when George Dorris and his wife Lulu bought 250 acres of fertile land along the Willamette River and dedicated their lives to farming. After experimenting with a variety of crops, George established the first commercial filbert nut orchard in the United States. Over the next 50 years, the Dorris family planted 9,200 trees at the ranch and harvested more than 50 tons of nuts each year.

Now, more than 100 years later, Dorris Ranch continues to make history as a fully productive commercial filbert orchard. More than half of all the commercial filbert trees now growing in the U.S. originated from Dorris Ranch nursery stock. I love hiking Dorris Ranch because most of it is flat and is next to the river.

PREs Trail- This is one of my favorites— okay, I know I say that about all of them but,... I walk this one almost every day with my dogs. The full trail is a 4.3-mile loop trail next to the Willamette River. It is flat and paved, it takes an average of 1 h 17 min to complete. You can start anywhere from Island Park in Springfield, to Alton Baker Park or beyond. Just head down towards the river and you cannot miss it.

We actually have had up to 13 nests in our rookery by the river. It is so awe-inspiring to watch the birds nest, hatch, feed, grow and take flight.

There are a variety of hikes in our beautiful area- I recommend searching
  https://www.alltrails.com/us/oregon/eugene for a list of more.

Biking Paradise

Eugene was made for bikes. Vertically every street has bike lanes. We encourage people to ride to work. I am not that brave but to each their own. We also have awesome bike paths for regular standard bikes, and electric and mountain bikes.

Another little-known fact is also known in the area as the **Ruth Bascom Riverbank Path System**. The trail follows the Willamette River from northeast Eugene to downtown Spring-field. The path is named after the late female mayor of Eugene who was a strong advocate for developing bicycle and pedestrian routes in the area. The path system connects many neighbor-hoods, city parks, and other outdoor riverside areas. It is all paved.

Start at Delta Highway River Trail Access point, then ride southwest on the East Bank path, continuing onto the South Bank path. You'll then cross the Knickerbocker Bridge Connec-tor to ride north on the South Bank Path, continuing on the West Bank Path. You'll then cross the Owosso Bridge Connector to head back towards the East Bank Path trailhead.

Hiking and Climbing

Skinner Butte Park: A Jewel of Eugene's Landscape

Location and Overview Nestled at 248 Cheshire Avenue, in the heart of Eugene, Oregon, Skinner Butte Park is more than just a green space; it's a vibrant slice of nature and history. This iconic park, spread across a vast area, serves as a serene getaway within the urban landscape of Eugene.

Historical Significance Skinner Butte Park holds a special place in the city's history. Named after Eugene Skinner, the founder of Eugene, the park and its commanding butte have been central to the community since the city's early days. The butte itself, rising prominently in the park, offers not just a glimpse into the region's past but also breathtaking views of the city and beyond.

Natural Beauty and Recreational Activities The park's natural beauty is a highlight, with lush greenery, beautifully maintained gardens, and scenic pathways. It's a popular spot for a range of activities – from leisurely walks and picnics to more energetic pursuits like rock climbing and biking. The bike path along the Willamette River is especially popular among cycling enthusiasts.

Family-Friendly Amenities Families frequent Skinner Butte Park for its excellent amenities. The playgrounds are modern and safe, providing endless entertainment for children. The park also features picnic areas, making it an ideal spot for family gatherings or a peaceful lunch amid nature.

The Climb to the Top For those seeking a bit of adventure, the climb to the top of Skinner Butte is a must. The trek is manageable and rewards climbers with panoramic views of Eugene. It's a favorite spot for photographers and nature lovers alike.

A Must-Visit Destination For anyone visiting or living in

Eugene, a trip to Skinner Butte Park is a must. It's not just a park; it's a vibrant part of Eugene's community, a place where nature, history, and recreation blend harmoniously. It's a testament to the beauty and spirit of Eugene, Oregon.

6

H2Oregon Discovering the Thrill of Water Adventures

Riverside Thrills and Chills: Oregon's Ultimate Water Adventures

Embark on a journey beyond the ordinary with Oregon's myriad of water-based activities. From the gentle tug of a fish on your line to the exhilarating rush of conquering whitewater rapids, the state's rivers and lakes offer endless opportunities for adventure and relaxation.

Dive into Oregon's Water Wonders: Fishing Excursions

Whether you're an experienced angler or a novice, Oregon's rivers and lakes are teeming with opportunities for fishing. Try fly fishing in tranquil streams or embark on a deep-sea fishing adventure in the Pacific. Each experience promises not just a catch, but a serene communion with nature.

Whitewater Rafting Thrills - For those seeking adrenaline-pumping excitement, Oregon's rivers provide some of the best whitewater rafting experiences. Navigate through roaring rapids, maneuver past boulders, and experience the thrill of the river's wild energy.

Kayaking and Canoeing - Explore Oregon's scenic waterways with a kayaking or canoeing trip. Glide through calm waters, paddle around lakes, or navigate gentle river currents. It's a peaceful way to experience the state's stunning landscapes from a different perspective.

Stand-up Paddleboarding (SUP) - Experience the growing sport of SUP on Oregon's calm lakes and gentle coastal waters. It's a fun way to enjoy the water while getting a full-body workout.

Scenic River Cruises - Enjoy a scenic river cruise for a more laid-back adventure. These excursions offer a relaxing way to appreciate Oregon's natural beauty, with stunning views and potential wildlife sightings.

Waterfall Chasing - Oregon's landscape is dotted with stunning waterfalls. Many of these natural wonders are accessible via water, offering a unique vantage point and the chance to experience their majestic beauty up close.

In Oregon, water isn't just a part of the landscape; it's a pathway to adventure. Each water-based activity offers a unique way to connect with the state's natural beauty, from the serene to the exhilarating. So grab your paddle, fishing rod, or rafting gear, and prepare for unforgettable aquatic adventures in Oregon's great outdoors.

River Trail Guides: Your Gateway to Outdoor Adventures Dive into the world of outdoor exploration with River Trail Guides, a premier adventure company based in Oregon. Specializing in guided tours along the region's scenic rivers and trails, River Trail Guides offers a range of experiences designed for outdoor enthusiasts of all levels. Whether you're seeking a tranquil river float or an exhilarating hiking adventure, they have something to satisfy every adventurer's spirit.

Exploring with River Trail Guides:

1. **Diverse Tour Offerings** - River Trail Guides provides a variety of guided tours including river rafting, kayaking, and canoeing, as well as hiking and camping trips. Each tour is thoughtfully planned to showcase the natural beauty and unique features of Oregon's landscapes.

2. **Expert Guides** - The company prides itself on its team of experienced and knowledgeable guides. These professionals are not only skilled in navigating the trails and waterways but are also passionate about sharing their love for the outdoors and the local ecology.

3. **Customizable Experiences** - Understanding that every group has different needs and interests, River Trail Guides offers customizable tours. Whether you're planning a family outing, a corporate team-building event, or a solo adventure, they can tailor an experience to meet your specific requirements.

4. **Safety and Instruction** - Safety is paramount on all their tours. River Trail Guides provides comprehensive safety briefings and instruction, ensuring that participants of all skill levels can enjoy their adventure with confidence.

5. **Access to Remote and Scenic Locations** - With their expert knowledge of the area, River Trail Guides takes you to some of the most beautiful and remote locations in Oregon. These are places often missed by casual visitors, offering a unique and immersive outdoor experience.

6. **Website:** For more information on available tours and bookings, visit www.RiverTrailGuides.com.

7. **Contact Number:** To speak with a representative or to make a reservation, call 541-953-9660.

8. **Educational Trips** - River Trail Guides also offers educational outings, perfect for schools or organizations interested in learning about the natural environment, conservation, and outdoor skills.

9. **Equipment Rentals** - For those who prefer to explore independently, they provide equipment rentals, including kayaks, canoes, and camping gear.

Choosing River Trail Guides for your next outdoor adventure means embarking on a journey filled with breathtaking scenery, exhilarating experiences, and memories that will last a lifetime. Whether you're paddling down a serene river, hiking through lush forests, or camping under the stars, their expertly guided tours promise an unforgettable encounter with the great outdoors.

Northwest Canoe Tour https://canoetour.org Rent Canoes, Kayaks & SUPs on Canoe Canal in Alton Baker Park info@canoetour.org The people who own this are amazing. They take the time to make sure you feel 100% comfortable before you shove off into the canal. This is great for kids as well as adults.

Cascade Adventures Company: Paddle Your Way to Fun Discover the joys of kayaking and paddle boarding with Cascade Adventures Company. Offering rentals for both kayaks and paddle boards, they are your go-to for aquatic adventures. Contact them at 541-556-5311, or visit www.CascadeAdventure Oregon.com for more information

Spencer Outfitters: Your Gateway to the Great Outdoors Spence Outfitters offers a wide range of outdoor activities and gear. Whether you're an experienced outdoorsman or new to outdoor adventures, they have something for everyone. Reach out at 425-286-4282, or explore www.SpencerOutfitters.com for more details.

Oregon Whitewater Adventures: Thrilling River Expeditions Embark on an exhilarating journey with Oregon Whitewater Adventures. Specializing in whitewater rafting, they provide thrilling river expeditions for all levels of adventurers. Contact them at 541-746-5422, or visit www.OregonWhiteWater.com for an unforgettable experience.

Home Waters Fly Fishing: Cast into Tranquility Home Waters Fly Fishing is a haven for fly fishing enthusiasts. Located at 444 W 3rd Ave, Eugene, OR 97401, they offer gear, advice, and guided trips. Call them at 541-342-6691 or visit www.homewatersflyfi shing.com for all your fly fishing needs.

Caddis Fly: Expert Guided Fly Fishing Trips Experience the best of fly fishing with Caddis Fly. They offer expertly guided trips for anglers of all levels. For more information, call 541-342-7005 or visit their blog at oregonflyfishingblog.com/guided-

<u>trips.</u>Each of these companies offers unique and exciting ways to explore Oregon's natural beauty. Whether you're paddling through serene waters, navigating thrilling rapids, or casting a line in a peaceful river, these adventures are sure to create lasting memories.

7

Pathways to Peace Oregon's Most Tranquil Garden Walks and Hikes

Gardens and Parks for a gentle walk surrounded by beauty

Hendricks Park is one of Eugene's oldest city parks. Located on the ridge line to the east of the University of Oregon, Hendricks Park was established in 1906. The 78-acre park, with its visible ridge line, is part of Eugene's identity.

The 78 acres of Hendricks Park contain the Rhododendron Garden (15 acres), the Native Plant Garden (5 acres), and the 58-acre forest. The accessible location of the park provides a popular area for runners, walkers, and others who simply want to stroll through the gardens.

This is an absolute must-see when you come to visit, especially if the Rhodys are in bloom.

Alton Baker Park, Eugene's largest developed park, has been an indispensable part of the Eugene landscape since 1959. Located right on the banks of the Willamette River directly across from the University of Oregon, Alton Baker has provided a place for locals of Eugene to bike, run, feed ducks, and take their dogs for over fifty years.

In the spring and summer, Alton Baker has its concert venue and has biking and walking trails that connect all over the Eugene and Springfield area, a canoe canal, a BMX track, a Disc Golf course, as well as an undeveloped and natural eastern section to the park, for those wishing to get away from civilization. Every weekend, something goes there, from Alzheimer's walks to Witches and Pagan fairs. I love to go and watch the ducks and geese in the ponds. Alton Baker Park consists of around 400 acres of forest, fields, plains, and trails and is a great place for relaxing, picnicking, and experiencing nature.

Owen Rose Garden 300 N. Jefferson St Eugene, OR 97401

The eight-and-a-half-acre park known as Owen Rose Garden is next to the Willamette River near the Washington Jefferson Street bridge. In 1951, George E. Owen, a former Eugene city councilor and lumberman, donated five acres with his house to the city. The Eugene Rose Society donated the original 750 rose bushes shortly after Owen donated the property. This original collection has expanded into a panorama of more than 4,500 roses of over 400 varieties. Stewardship by many volunteers has continued, including the Delta Rotary, who from 1999 to 2004 spearheaded a major renovation of the garden.

Little known fact:

The rose garden features the nationally recognized Oregon Heritage Cherry Tree, a 28-foot-diameter gazebo, an arbor picnic area, a parking lot and maintenance facility, and an impressive collection of heritage and heirloom roses. It is a beautiful walk on any day.

20x21 Mural Project: Transforming Eugene's Urban Canvas

The 20x21 Mural Project, an ambitious initiative under the City of Eugene Cultural Service's Public Art Program, aimed to enrich Eugene's urban landscape with more than 20 world-class outdoor murals by the 2022 IAAF World Championships. This innovative project was an artistic endeavor and a collaborative effort that brought together various community sectors, including communications, law, architecture, small business, nonprofits, and the arts.

Elevating Eugene through Art:

1. **Global Artistic Collaboration** - The project sought to infuse Eugene's cityscape with global perspectives by inviting renowned artists worldwide. These artists contributed unique styles and cultural influences, turning the city's walls into a vibrant, international art gallery.

2. **Fostering Community Pride and Identity** - By transforming blank walls into dynamic works of art, the 20x21 Mural Project aimed to promote community pride and contribute to Eugene's identity. Each mural tells a story, reflects community values, and adds to the city's cultural fabric.

3. **Enhancing Urban Aesthetics** - The murals, strategically located across the city, beautified Eugene's urban areas and stimulated cultural and economic growth. They became focal points for community gatherings, tourism, and cultural dialogues.

4. **Educational and Cultural Exchange—An essential goal of the project was to create opportunities for artist exchanges. This facet of the program allowed Eugene artists to engage with international cities, fostering a global cultural exchange and broadening the artistic horizons** of local creators.

5. **Interactive Art Tours—The project enriched Eugene's cultural tourism, with guided and self-guided mural tours becoming popular activities** for locals and visitors alike. These tours offered insights into the stories behind the murals and the artists who created them.

Legacy and Impact:

- The 20x21 Mural Project has left a lasting legacy in Eugene, transforming the city into a canvas that narrates diverse stories through art. Its impact goes beyond aesthetics, contributing to the city's cultural, social, and economic vitality.

· The project has inspired similar initiatives in other cities, showcasing the power of public art in community building and urban rejuvenation.

The 20x21 Mural Project is a testament to art's transformative power in public spaces. By turning the city into a vibrant gallery of world-class murals, Eugene has enhanced its urban landscape, strengthened its community bonds, celebrated diversity, and positioned itself as a cultural landmark in the Pacific Northwest.

I highly recommend you go to their website for more information, including maps of current murals; please go to https://www.eugene-or.gov/3492/20x21-Mural-Project , what we have created in Eugene and Springfield is masterful in making you stop and stare.

8

Unique and Fun Destinations in Eugene and Springfield

Jordan Schnitzer Museum of Art - Immerse yourself in a world of artistic wonder at the Jordan Schnitzer Museum of Art. This museum is not just a place to view art; it's an experience that takes you through diverse cultures and histories. From ancient artifacts to contemporary masterpieces, the museum's vast collection is a testament to the power of visual storytelling. Visit the website for current exhibitions https://jsma.uoregon.edu/

Oregon Air and Space Museum - Take to the skies with a visit to the Oregon Air and Space Museum. This museum offers an intriguing glimpse into the world of aviation and space exploration. Here, you can explore a wide array of aircraft and spacecraft, learn about the science of flight, and discover the stories of pioneers who dared to reach for the stars. http://www.oasmuseum.com/

Science Factory Children's Museum and Planetarium - Spark your child's curiosity at the Science Factory Children's Museum and Planetarium. This interactive museum is a playground of learning, where children can engage with hands-on exhibits and delve into the wonders of science. The planetarium adds to the excitement, offering a mesmerizing journey through the cosmos. For more information, call 541-682-7888 or explore their universe online at https://eugenesciencecenter.org/pla netarium/. This educational adventure promises to ignite a lifelong passion for discovery in young minds

The Museum of Natural and Cultural History: A Portal to the Past, Present, and Future

The Museum of Natural and Cultural History, located in the heart of Eugene stands as a beacon of learning and discovery. It's not just a museum; it's a dynamic space where connections are forged between people, our collective past, and the possibilities of our future. Here, science and culture intertwine, offering visitors a rich tapestry of experiences and knowledge.

Explore the Depths of History and Culture:

1. **Scientific Exploration** - The museum is renowned for its extensive scientific exhibits. From geology and paleontology to biology and environmental science, it offers a deep dive into the natural world. Interactive exhibits allow visitors to engage with scientific concepts and understand the processes shaping our planet.

2. **Cultural Celebrations** - The museum also celebrates the rich tapestry of human culture. It showcases the diverse histories, arts, and traditions of people from around the world, with a special emphasis on local and regional cultures. Through artifacts, art, and storytelling, visitors gain a deeper appreciation of our shared human experience.

3. **Educational Programs and Events** - The museum is a hub of educational activity, hosting a variety of programs, workshops, and events for all ages. These include lectures by experts, hands-on educational workshops, and special events that bring the community together to learn and celebrate.

4. **Focus on Sustainability and Justice** - Central to the museum's mission is the promotion of a just and sustainable world. It encourages dialogue and action on critical issues like climate change, conservation, and social justice, inspiring visitors to become active participants in shaping a better future.

5. **Visitor Information**

- **Location:** The Museum of Natural and Cultural History is located on the University of Oregon campus in Eugene, at 1680 East 15th Avenue Eugene, OR 97403
- **Contact:** For more information about current exhibits, and programs, or to plan a visit, call the museum or check their website at https://mnch.uoregon.edu/visit

Adventure Children's Museum: A World of Learning and Fun

Embark on an educational journey at the Adventure Children's Museum, located at 490 Valley River Center, Eugene, OR 97401. This interactive and engaging museum is dedicated to sparking curiosity and fostering a love of learning in children of all ages.

Interactive Exhibits - The museum features a variety of hands-on exhibits that encourage children to explore, play, and learn.

These exhibits cover a range of topics from science and nature to culture and the arts, making learning both fun and immersive.

1. **Educational Programs** - Adventure Children's Museum offers an array of educational programs, including workshops, classes, and special events. These programs are designed to complement the exhibits and provide deeper learning opportunities for children.
2. **Family-Friendly Environment** - The museum is designed to be a family-friendly space where children and their caregivers can engage in activities together. It's a safe and welcoming environment for families to spend quality time while learning and exploring.
3. **Special Events and Activities** - Regularly hosting special events and activities, the museum provides unique experiences like storytelling sessions, arts and crafts workshops, and science demonstrations that are both educational and entertaining.

Visit them at adventurechildrensmuseum.org. to find to discover what exhibits are currently showing.

Visiting the Adventure Children's Museum is more than just a day out; it's an adventure into a world of imagination and discovery. With its hands-on exhibits and educational programs, the museum is where children can learn about the world around them in a fun, interactive environment. It's an ideal destination for families looking for an educational and enjoyable activity in Eugene.

Emerald Art Center: A Hub of Creativity and Community in

Springfield

Nestled in the heart of Springfield at 500 Main St, the Emerald Art Center is a vibrant community space dedicated to nurturing creativity and fostering an appreciation for the arts. This dynamic center is not just an art gallery; it's a place where artists, art enthusiasts, and the community converge to celebrate and engage with the visual arts.

Exhibitions and Galleries – The center showcases an array of exhibitions throughout the year, featuring works by local and regional artists. The exhibitions provide a diverse view of artistic expression from contemporary art to traditional mediums.

Workshops and Classes – Emerald Art Center is committed to art education for all ages and skill levels. They offer a range of classes and workshops led by experienced artists, covering various mediums, including painting, drawing, and photography.

1. **Community Events** – The center hosts several community events, including artist talks, gallery walks, and receptions, offering opportunities for the public to interact with artists and learn more about their processes and inspirations.

2. **Support for Local Artists** – Emerald Art Center is a platform for local artists to showcase their work, network with other artists, and engage with the community.

3. **Art Resources** – The center also offers resources for artists, including studio space, art supplies, and a library of art books, making it a valuable asset for both emerging and established artists.

4. **Art Sales and Gift Shop** – Visitors can purchase original artworks and handcrafted items from the center's sales gallery and gift shop, supporting local artists and artisans.

Visitor Information:

- **Location:** 500 Main St, Springfield, OR 97477.
- **Contact:** To learn more about current exhibitions, classes, or events, call (541) 726-8595 or visit emeraldartcenter.org.

The Emerald Art Center is more than just an art center; it's a cultural beacon in Springfield, inviting everyone to explore, appreciate, and participate in the art world. Whether you're an artist seeking inspiration, a student eager to learn, or simply someone who appreciates the beauty of art, the Emerald Art Center offers a welcoming space to indulge in the rich tapestry of visual arts.

Hayward Field: A Hallowed Ground of Athletics and Inspiration

Hayward Field, located at the University of Oregon in Eugene, is more than just a track and field stadium. It's a hallowed ground, a repository of athletic history, and a symbol of the enduring spirit of sportsmanship. As one of the world's most renowned track and field venues, Hayward Field has hosted many significant events, from national championships to international competitions, including the prestigious Olympic Trials.

Immersing in the Legacy of Hayward Field:

1. **Rich Athletic History** - Hayward Field's legacy dates back over a century, having been a focal point for track and field since its inception in 1919. This storied stadium has witnessed the rise of numerous track and field stars and groundbreaking athletic feats, making it a pilgrimage site for sports enthusiasts.

2. **State-of-the-Art Renovation** - The recent renovation of Hayward Field has transformed it into a world-class athletic facility while preserving its rich history. The new design includes advanced training and competition spaces, a spectator-friendly layout, and cutting-edge amenities that elevate the athletic experience.

3. **Tributes to Track and Field Legends** - The stadium houses displays and exhibits that pay tribute to track and field legends. Visitors can explore the sport's rich history through these exhibits, gaining insight into the lives and accomplishments of some of the greatest athletes.

4. **Architectural Marvel** - Beyond its athletic significance, Hayward Field is an architectural marvel. The stadium's design is functional and aesthetically pleasing, blending seamlessly into the University of Oregon's campus while standing out as a modern sports venue.

5. **Venue for Major Events** - Hayward Field remains a preferred venue for major track and field events, drawing athletes and spectators from around the globe. Its state-of-the-art facilities provide an ideal setting for high-profile competitions.

6. **Community and University Engagement** - The stadium is a hub for community events and university activities. It's a place where the local community and university students come together to celebrate sports and partake in various events.

Visitor Information:

- **Location:** University of Oregon, Eugene, OR. Even Hayward Field's street address honors history. Set at 1530 Agate

St., the numbers recognize the time of 1:53.0, Phil Knight's personal best in the 800 meters.

Explore the Venue: Visitors are welcome to explore Hayward Field, though access may vary depending on events and university schedules. It's recommended to check ahead for public access times and tour availability on their website https://hayward.uoregon.edu/

Why Visit Hayward Field:

- **Inspiring Atmosphere** - The energy and spirit of athletics are palpable at Hayward Field. Its venue inspires visitors with its history, achievements, and dedication to the sport of track and field.
- **Educational Experience** - For aspiring athletes, sports enthusiasts, and history buffs, Hayward Field offers an educational journey through the evolution of track and field, highlighting the achievements and challenges of the sport.

Visiting Hayward Field is an experience that transcends the ordinary. It's an opportunity to connect with the legacy of track and field, to be inspired by the stories of athletes who have competed here, and to witness the evolution of a sport that continues to captivate and thrill audiences worldwide. Hayward Field is not just a stadium; it's a testament to the enduring spirit of athleticism and the pursuit of excellence.

Matthew Knight Arena: A Modern Marvel in Eugene's Sports and Entertainment Scene

Matthew Knight Arena, prominently located in Eugene, Oregon, is a state-of-the-art multipurpose arena that serves as a centerpiece for sports, entertainment, and cultural events. Named in honor of Matthew Knight, the late son of Nike co-founder Phil Knight, the arena is known for its cutting-edge design, advanced technology, and vibrant atmosphere.

Highlights of Matthew Knight Arena:

1. **Home to Oregon Ducks Basketball** - The arena is the proud home of the University of Oregon's basketball team, the Oregon Ducks. It provides an electrifying environment for college basketball games, with a seating capacity of over 12,000, ensuring every game is a memorable experience for players and fans alike.

2. **Innovative Design and Features** - Matthew Knight Arena stands out for its modern architecture and innovative features. The interior boasts one of the most distinctive court designs in college basketball, known for its intricate representation of a fir tree forest, symbolizing Oregon's lush landscapes.

3. **Versatile Venue for Events** - Beyond basketball, the arena hosts various events, including concerts, family shows, commencement ceremonies, and cultural events. Its versatile design allows for easy transformation to suit different events, making it Eugene's entertainment hub.

4. **State-of-the-Art Facilities** - The arena has advanced sound and lighting systems, large video screens, and comfortable seating designed to enhance the visitor experience. Whether it's a sports event or a concert, guests are assured a high-quality, immersive experience.

5. **Sustainability** - Reflecting Oregon's environmental commitment, Matthew Knight Arena incorporates sustainable

practices in its operations, including energy-efficient systems and environmentally friendly materials.

Visitor Information:

- **Location:** 1776 E 13th Ave, Eugene, OR 97403.

Contact: For information about upcoming events, tickets, or general inquiries, visitors can call the arena or visit its website at https://goducks.com/feature/mka

Why Visit Matthew Knight Arena:

- **Experience High-Energy Sports** - For sports fans, especially basketball enthusiasts, attending a game at the arena is necessary. The crowd's energy and the game's thrill create an unforgettable atmosphere.
- **Top-Tier Entertainment** - With a lineup of concerts and events featuring renowned artists and entertainers, the arena is a key destination for those who enjoy top-tier entertainment in Eugene.
- **Architectural Appreciation** - The arena's unique design and features make it a point of interest for those who appreciate modern architecture and innovative design in public spaces.

Matthew Knight Arena is more than just a sports venue; it's a landmark of Eugene's cultural and entertainment landscape. Whether you're cheering on the Ducks, enjoying a concert, or attending a special event, the arena promises an experience filled with excitement, innovation, and the spirit of Oregon.

Aragon Alpacas

Ann and Mike Dockendorf are the passionate proprietors of Aragon Alpacas, located at 33005 Dillard Road in Eugene, Oregon. Established in 2005, Aragon Alpacas represents the culmination of Ann and Mike's dream, which began while living in the city. Initially boarding their growing herd, the couple acquired a vintage farm near Eugene to provide a permanent home for their alpacas.

Aragon Alpacas is not just a farm; it's a center for community education and engagement in the world of alpacas. Ann is actively involved in the mentoring and support of alpaca owners and enthusiasts through local camelid associations. Ann shares her extensive knowledge and appreciation of alpacas as eco-friendly livestock by hosting farm tours, offering visitors a unique and immersive experience.

The farm itself is a testament to the couple's dedication to their alpacas, showcasing the careful breeding and nurturing of the Huacaya alpacas. The Dockendorfs harvest the fine fleece of these animals annually, making it available to hand-crafters in various forms, including raw fleece, roving for spinners, batting for quilts, and yarn. Their commitment to sustainable and ethical animal husbandry and agriculture practices is evident in every aspect of their operation.

Visitors to Aragon Alpacas can expect a warm welcome and an enriching experience. The farm offers a chance to meet the alpacas up close, learn about their care, and appreciate the beauty and versatility of their fleece. The serene setting of the farm, combined with the Dockendorfs' hospitality and expertise, makes Aragon Alpacas a must-visit destination for anyone interested in sustainable farming, animal husbandry, or simply looking for a unique and educational outing in the Eugene area.

For more information about Aragon Alpacas, their events, and farm tours, visit their website at http://aragonalpacas.com or call 541-912-0782.

Get Air Eugene: A World of Excitement and Fun

An Adventure for All Ages Get Air Eugene, located at 4211 W. 11th Ave in Eugene, Oregon, is not just another trampoline park; it's a vibrant hub of activity, excitement, and joy. From wall-to-wall trampolines to many dynamic activities, this indoor amusement center promises an unforgettable experience for visitors of all ages. Whether you're looking to host a memorable birthday party, enjoy a family outing, or have a blast with friends, Get Air Eugene offers the perfect setting. With its commitment to safety and fun, every jump, flip, and bounce is an adventure.

Diverse and Engaging Activities This trampoline park takes fun to new heights with its extensive range of activities. The facility boasts a Kiddie Court, specially designed for the little ones under 46 inches, ensuring they can enjoy the excitement in a safe environment. For those seeking a bit of competition, the trampoline dodgeball arena adds a thrilling twist to the classic game. Adventure seekers can also experience the exhilaration of soaring through the air and landing into a giant foam pit. The park's unique attractions, such as slam ball and ninja obstacles, cater to various interests, making every visit a discovery.

Special Events and Accessibility Get Air Eugene is dedicated to inclusivity and accessibility. It offers special events like Toddler Time, where parents and their little ones can enjoy the park, and dedicated times for special-needs jumpers. Club Air nights transform the park into a lively party atmosphere with music and lights every Friday and Saturday night. The park's versatility makes it an ideal venue for group events, team sports, corporate gatherings, and family reunions. With its commitment to providing a fun, safe, and inclusive environment, Get Air Eugene stands out as a premier destination for indoor recreation and entertainment in the Eugene area.

Check out their website at: https://getairsports.com/shop/eugene/

Make a Difference with Your Review

Unlock the Power of Generosity

"Money can't buy happiness, but giving it away can." - Freddie Mercury.

Folks say if you give without expecting anything back, you'll be happier, live longer, and even have a few extra bucks. Count me in if there's even a sliver of a chance for that! So, here's what I'm thinking...

Imagine doing something super cool for someone you've never met without wanting a pat. Who is this mystery person, you ask? Well, they're a bit like you, or at least how you were once upon a time—eager to explore, ready to make a mark, and on the lookout for that guiding light but not quite sure where to find it.

Our big goal is to make the wonders of Visiting Eugene-Springfield something anyone can experience. Everything I do is all about hitting that goal. And the only way to make that dream a reality is to spread the word to everyone.

And here's where you come in! Many people judge a book by its cover—or its reviews, to be exact. So, I'm reaching out to ask for a little favor on behalf of a fellow explorer you haven't met yet:

Could you take a moment to leave a review for this book?

It won't cost you a dime and take less than a minute, but your words could open a new world for another reader. Your review might help...

...another small business thrives in its community.

...an entrepreneur supports their family with pride.

...someone lands a job that fills their life with purpose.

...a client finds that life-changing spark.

...make someone's dream a reality.

And all it takes to spread that joy is a quick review. Ready to feel awesome and make a real difference? Just scan the QR code below to leave your review:

If the thought of helping out a fellow Eugene-Springfield enthusiast brings a smile to your face, then you're my kind of person. Welcome to the club; you're one of the good ones.

I can't wait to share more about how you can dive deeper into the heart of Eugene-Springfield, discovering secrets and strategies that will make your journey even more magical. You're gonna love what's in store.

A huge thank you from the very bottom of my heart. Now, let's jump back into our adventure.

• Your biggest fan, Helen Williams

P.S. – Did you know? When you share something valuable, you become even more valuable to others. If this guide can help another explorer like you, why not spread the love and send this book their way?

9

Unveiling the Past A Tour of Eugene's Historical Sites

Each of these historical sites in Eugene offers a unique window into different aspects of the city's rich heritage. Whether it's through the elegance of Victorian architecture, the rustic charm of a working farm, or the competitive spirit of a world-class athletic stadium, these landmarks provide a tangible connection to the stories that have shaped Eugene.

Dorris Ranch Living Historical Farm

Explore the roots of Oregon's farming heritage at Dorris Ranch Living Historical Farm. This working farm, a blend of history and nature, invites visitors to experience early 20th-century farm life. The ranch features original buildings, including a farmhouse, barn, and schoolhouse, each carefully maintained to reflect their historical significance. Walking through the orchards and along the scenic trails, one can almost hear the echoes of the past, offering a serene escape into rural history. Located at 205 Dorris Street in Springfield, OR 97477.

Shelton-McMurphey-Johnson House -

Step back in time at the Shelton-McMurphey-Johnson House, a stunning Victorian-era mansion perched on a hill overlooking Eugene. This beautifully preserved house, adorned with intricate architectural details, offers a glimpse into the opulent lifestyle of the late 19th century. Each room tells a story, filled with period furnishings and personal artifacts that belonged to the three families who once called it home. The house also hosts various cultural events and themed teas, providing a living connection to the past. 303 Willamette St. Eugene, OR For more information check out the website at: https://smjhouse.org. located at 303 Willamette Street Eugene, OR 97401. Enter the Driveway at Third and Pearl Streets.

Springfield History Museum: A Window into the Heart of Oregon

Nestled in the bustling Main Street of Springfield, Oregon, at 590 Main St, the Springfield History Museum is a hidden gem waiting to be discovered. This museum is not just a building filled with artifacts; it's a vibrant storyteller, a keeper of the city's soul, and a testament to the rich tapestry of Springfield's past.

Housed in the iconic Springfield Power and Water building, the museum itself is a piece of history. The building, constructed in the early 20th century, stands as a relic of Springfield's industrial age, its architecture reflecting the era's style and spirit. This historic setting provides the perfect backdrop for a journey through time.

Inside, the museum is a treasure trove of stories and memories. Each exhibit is carefully curated to offer visitors an intimate glimpse into the lives of Springfield's early settlers, the town's development over the years, and the culture that shaped it. From historical photographs, documents, and artifacts to interactive displays, the museum provides a comprehensive and engaging exploration of Springfield's heritage.

One of the unique aspects of the Springfield History Museum is its focus on the local community. It doesn't just tell a generic story of a town; it delves into the personal, intimate tales of the people who built Springfield. It's a place where visitors can learn about the pioneers, the loggers, the mill workers, and the everyday citizens who have all played a role in shaping the city.

Special exhibitions often highlight specific aspects of Springfield's history, from its natural environment and indigenous cultures to its evolution into a modern city. The museum also actively engages with the community, hosting educational programs, workshops, and events that bring the city's history to life for people of all ages.

For anyone looking to understand Springfield's heart and soul, the Springfield History Museum is an essential visit. It's a place where history is not just remembered but vividly alive, continually educating and inspiring those who walk through its doors. This museum is not just about the past; it's about connecting the past to the present and future, making it a vital part of Springfield's ongoing story.

It's best to check out the website to make sure they will be open. https://wheremindsgrow.org/your_library/museum

10

Eugene's Flourishing Art, Music, and Entertainment Scene

Eugene Symphony

- **Description:** A cultural gem, the Eugene Symphony enchants with its range of symphonic music, from classical masterpieces to contemporary compositions.

Contact: (541) 687-9487
For current concerts https://eugenesymphony.org

- **Location:** Hult Center for the Performing Arts, Eugene, OR

Studio West Glassblowing Studio

- **Description:** Studio West is a creative haven where visitors can witness the transformation of molten glass into exquisite art, participate in workshops, and learn the craft.
- **Contact:** (541) 342-9428 or visit at https://visitstudiowest.com/

- **Location:** 245 W 8th Ave, Eugene, OR 97401

Tsunami Books

- **Description:** More than a bookstore, Tsunami Books is a vibrant community hub for literature, hosting author readings, poetry nights, and musical performances. Plus is just a cool place to spend hours in.
- **Contact:** (541) 345-8986 or visit https://www.tsunamibooks.org/
- **Location:** 2585 Willamette St, Eugene, OR 97405

Hult Center for the Performing Arts

- **Description:** The epicenter of Eugene's performing arts, the Hult Center hosts a variety of performances from ballet and opera to Broadway shows.
- **Contact:** (541) 682-5000 or for up-to-date information visit https://hultcenter.org/
- **Location:** 1 Eugene Center, Eugene, OR 97401

WOW Hall

- **Description:** A historic venue with an eclectic mix of music, the WOW Hall is a beloved space for live music, showcasing everything from indie bands to world music.
- **Contact:** (541) 687-2746 or visit https://wowhall.org/
- **Location:** 291 W 8th Ave, Eugene, OR 97401
-

Very Little Theater

- **Description:** One of the oldest community theaters, the Very Little Theater presents a diverse array of plays and musicals, highlighting local talent.
- **Contact:** (541) 344-7751 or visit https://thevlt.com/
- **Location:** 2350 Hilyard St, Eugene, OR 97405

Richard E Wildish Community Theater

- **Description:** Located in Springfield, this intimate venue offers a mix of plays, concerts, and dance performances.
- **Contact:** (541) 868-0689 or visit https://www.wildishtheater.com/
- **Location:** 630 Main St, Springfield, OR 97477

Actors Cabaret of Eugene

- **Description:** Enjoy a unique blend of dinner and musical theater at Actors Cabaret, known for its captivating productions.
- **Contact:** (541) 683-4368 or visit https://www.actorscabaret.org/
- **Location:** 996 Willamette St, Eugene, OR 97401

Oregon Contemporary Theater

- **Description:** This theater is a hub for modern plays and innovative performances, often focusing on contemporary themes.
- **Contact:** (541) 465-1506 or visit https://www.octheatre.org/
- **Location:** 194 W Broadway, Eugene, OR 97401

McDonald Theater

- **Description:** A historic venue, McDonald Theater hosts concerts, comedy shows, and other performances, making it a must-visit for entertainment seekers.
- **Contact:** (541) 345-4442 or visit https://mcdonaldtheatre.com/
- **Location:** 1010 Willamette St, Eugene, OR 97401

University Theater

- **Description:** On the University of Oregon campus, this theater showcases student and faculty talent in a range of productions.
- **Contact:** (541) 346-4363 or visit https://blogs.uoregon.edu/theatre/
- **Location:** University of Oregon, Eugene, OR

Cuthbert Amphitheater

- **Description:** An open-air venue for summer concerts and festivals, surrounded by nature. They have had some amazing concerts. It is an experience to sit on the grass and listen to the sounds all around you.
- **Contact:** (541) 762-8099
- **Location:** 601 Day Island Rd, Eugene, OR 97401

The Shedd Institute: A Cultural Beacon in Eugene's Art Scene

The Shedd Institute, located at 868 High Street in Eugene, Oregon, is a vibrant center for the arts and an integral part of the city's cultural landscape. Known simply as "The Shedd," this institution is dedicated to nurturing and promoting the performing arts, offering a diverse array of artistic experiences to the community. **Dive into the World of Performing Arts at The Shedd:**

1. **Music and Theater Performances** - The Shedd is renowned for its wide range of musical and theatrical productions. From jazz concerts and classical recitals to musical theater and contemporary performances, the institute's programming caters to a variety of artistic tastes.

2. **Educational Programs** - A cornerstone of The Shedd's mission is education. The institute offers an array of educational programs, workshops, and classes for all ages and skill levels. Whether it's music lessons, vocal training, or theater arts, The Shedd provides opportunities for community members to learn and grow as artists.

3. **Community Engagement and Outreach** - The Shedd actively engages with the Eugene community through outreach programs, school collaborations, and special community events. These initiatives aim to make the arts accessible to a wider audience and to foster a love of the arts in the community.

4. **Architectural Charm** - The building itself, a fixture in downtown Eugene, adds to the institute's allure. Its historic architecture and well-designed performance spaces create an inviting and intimate atmosphere for audience members.

5. **Diverse Event Hosting—In addition to its programming, The Shedd hosts various** events, including community gatherings, private events, and other cultural activities. The institute's facilities are available for rent, providing a

unique and elegant setting for various occasions.

- **Visitor Information:**
- **Location:** 868 High Street, Eugene, OR.
- **Contact:** For information about upcoming events, ticketing, or educational programs, call (541) 434-7000. or visit https://theshedd.org/

- **Why Visit The Shedd Institute:**
- **Rich Artistic Experience**—The Shedd offers an immersive artistic experience with performances and programs that enrich Eugene's cultural life.
- Participation and Learning Opportunities - For those looking to participate in the arts, The Shedd's educational programs offer a chance to learn from experienced instructors in a supportive environment.
- **Cultural Gathering Place** - The institute serves as a gathering place for the community, where people can come together to enjoy and celebrate the performing arts.
- The Shedd Institute stands as a testament to Eugene's dedication to the arts. Whether you're an aspiring artist, a seasoned performer, or a lover of the arts, The Shedd provides a space to engage with and be inspired by the vibrant world of music and theater.

1st Friday Art Walk - Eugene

- **Description:** A monthly celebration of local art, with galleries opening their doors for special exhibits and events. This free event often allows you to enjoy the art and talk with the local artists.

- **Location:** Downtown Eugene, OR visit https://lanearts.org/first-friday-artwalk/

2nd Friday Art Walk - Springfield

- **Description:** Experience the art scene of Springfield with this event showcasing local artists. Just as Eugene does, you will get an up close and personal view of the amazing talent we have right here in Oregon.
- **Location:** Springfield, OR, or visit https://www.emeraldartcenter.org/second-friday

Each venue and event embodies Eugene and Springfield's creative spirit, creating a rich tapestry of art, music, and entertainment that enlivens the city's soul. Whether you're a lover of the arts, an avid reader, a theater enthusiast, or a concertgoer, there's something in this vibrant community to captivate and inspire you.

Battle Axe - Test your aim at Battle Axe, located at 303 S. 5th Street, Suite 147 in the Booth Kelly Center.in Springfield. This unique venue offers an exhilarating experience of axe throwing. For details, visit oregonaxethrowing.com or call 541-726-3836.

Portal Adventures - Escape Rooms - Challenge your problem-solving skills at Portal Adventures in Springfield. These escape rooms offer immersive and thrilling adventures for groups. Located at 2237 Main St. Ste 2, Springfield, OR 97477, you can call (541) 780-6180 or visit portaladventures.com for bookings.

Trap Door - Dive into the mystery at Trap Door, Eugene's intriguing escape room experience. They can be reached at 436 Charnelton St Ste 101, Eugene, OR 97401 at (541) 937-5063 or trapdooreugene.com.

Mental Mansions - Mental Mansion Escape Rooms in Eugene offers a captivating escape room experience. Find them at 1849 Willamette St, Eugene, OR 97401, call (541) 357-5090, or visit https://www.mentalmansion.com/

Camp Putt Adventure Park Mini Golf - Enjoy a day of family fun at Camp Putt Adventure Park Mini Golf. Located at 4006 Franklin Blvd, Eugene, OR 97403, this mini-golf course promises fun for all ages. Call +1 541 852 4653 or visit https://willamalane.org/places/camp-putt for more information.

MultiVRse VR Gaming - Step into the future with VR gaming at MultiVRse. This virtual reality gaming center offers a range of immersive games and experiences. Find them at 2001 Franklin Blvd, Eugene, OR 97403, call 541-221-5172, visit https://multivrse.games/

Eugene Food Tours - Eugene Eats - Discover the culinary delights of Eugene with Eugene Food Tours. A guided gastronomic adventure awaits. Visit eugenefoodtours.com or call 541-357-7992 for more details.

Art with Alejandro - Explore your creative side with Art with

Alejandro. Offering art classes and workshops, it's a great place to learn and create. Located at 590 Pearl St Suite 104, Eugene, OR, contact them at 541-554-4414 or Alejandro@artwithalejandro.com.

Top Golf Indoor Golf at Graduate Eugene - Swing into action at Top Golf Indoor Golf, situated within Graduate Eugene. For a unique golfing experience, call (541) 342-2000 x6659 or visit https://graduatehotels.com/eugene/topgolf

The Potters Quarter: Unleashing Creativity in Clay Pottery

Exploring The Potters Quarter Open Studio Time The Potters Quarter, located at 2848 Willamette St, Eugene, OR 97405, is a creative haven for pottery enthusiasts and beginners alike. This pottery studio and gallery is a vibrant space where individuals can explore the art of ceramics, nurture their creativity, and create unique pieces of art.

- **Family and Group Activities**—The studio is perfect for family activities, group outings, or team-building events. Pottery-making is a fun and creative experience and a great way to bond and create lasting memories.

Location: 2848 Willamette St, Eugene, OR 97405.

Contact: To learn more, call (541) 434-9277 or visit https://www.pottersquarter.com/

Onsen Hot Tub and Sauna: A Haven of Relaxation in Eugene

Nestled in the picturesque setting of Eugene, Oregon, Onsen Hot Tub and Sauna offers a serene escape from the hustle and bustle of daily life. Located at 1883 Garden Avenue, this tranquil facility is perfect for those seeking relaxation and rejuvenation.
Unwind and Rejuvenate at Onsen:

1. **Private Hot Tub Experience** - Onsen provides private hot tub rooms where guests can enjoy a peaceful soak in a calm, relaxing environment. The hot tubs are meticulously maintained, ensuring a clean and safe experience for all guests.
2. **Soothing Sauna Sessions** - In addition to hot tubs, Onsen offers sauna facilities. The dry heat of the sauna is ideal for relaxing muscles, detoxifying the body, and providing a moment of quiet reflection.
3. **Health and Wellness Benefits** - Both hot tub soaking and sauna sessions offer numerous health benefits, including stress reduction, improved circulation, and relief from muscle aches and pains. It's a holistic wellness approach that rejuvenates the body and mind.
4. **Serene and Comfortable Setting** - The facility is designed to provide a tranquil and comfortable experience. The serene setting and the warm, welcoming atmosphere make Onsen an oasis of relaxation.
5. **Reservation System for Convenience** - To ensure a personalized and uninterrupted experience, Onsen operates on a reservation system. Guests are encouraged to call ahead to book their hot tub or sauna session, allowing for a tailored visit suited to their schedule and preferences.

- **Visitor Information:**

- **Location:** 1883 Garden Avenue, Eugene, Oregon.
- **Contact:** For reservations or more information about the facilities and services, call (541) 345-9048. or visit https://www.onsenspas.com

Onsen Hot Tub and Sauna is more than just a wellness facility; it's a sanctuary where one can find peace, relaxation, and a momentary pause from the outside world. It's an ideal destination for anyone looking to indulge in the therapeutic benefits of hot tub soaking and sauna, all within Eugene, Oregon's beautiful and serene surroundings.

Get Air Eugene: A World of Excitement and Fun

An Adventure for All Ages Get Air Eugene, located at 4211 W. 11th Ave in Eugene, Oregon, is not just another trampoline park; it's a vibrant hub of activity, excitement, and joy. From wall-to-wall trampolines to a plethora of dynamic activities, this indoor amusement center promises an unforgettable experience for visitors of all ages. Whether you're looking to host a memorable birthday party, enjoy a family outing, or simply have a blast with friends, Get Air Eugene offers the perfect setting. With its commitment to safety and fun, every jump, flip, and bounce is an adventure in itself.

Diverse and Engaging Activities This trampoline park takes fun to new heights with its extensive range of activities. The facility boasts a Kiddie Court, specially designed for the little ones under 46 inches, ensuring they can enjoy the excitement in a safe environment. For those seeking a bit of competition, the trampoline dodgeball arena adds a thrilling twist to the classic game. Adventure seekers can also experience the exhilaration of soaring through the air and landing into a giant foam pit. The park's unique attractions, such as slam ball and ninja obstacles, cater to various interests, making every visit a discovery.

Special Events and Accessibility Get Air Eugene is dedicated to inclusivity and accessibility. It offers special events like Toddler Time, where parents and their little ones can enjoy the park, and dedicated times for special-needs jumpers. Club Air nights transform the park into a lively party atmosphere with music and lights every Friday and Saturday night. The park's versatility makes it an ideal venue for group events, team sports, corporate gatherings, and family reunions. With its commitment to providing a fun, safe, and inclusive environment, Get Air Eugene stands out as a premier destination for indoor recreation and entertainment in the Eugene area.

11

Swimming-Bowling and Beyond

Swimming Facilities:

Willamalane Park Swim Center.1276 G St, Springfield, OR 97477 Call 541-736-4544 for more info. or visit https://www.willamal ane.org/facilities/willamalane_park_swim_center/index.php

This is an Indoor Facility.

Splash! At Lively Park - A fun and family-friendly water park located at 6100 Thurston Road, Springfield, OR 97478. call 541-736-4244 or visit https://www.willamalane.org/facilities/splas h!_at_lively_park/index.php.

This is an Indoor Facility.

River Road Park & Recreation District - Offering swimming facilities at 1400 Lake Dr. Eugene, OR 97404. Call 541-461-7777 or visit rrpark.org.

This is an Indoor Facility.

Amazon Pool - A popular public pool located at 2600 Hilyard St. Eugene, OR 97405. Phone: 541-682-5350 or visit eugene-or.gov/3223/Amazon-Pool.

This is an outside Pool and may be closed due to weather, call ahead.

Each of these destinations offers a unique and entertaining experience, perfect for exploring the fun and whimsical side of Eugene and Springfield. Whether it's unleashing your artistic talents, embarking on an immersive game, or enjoying a leisurely day of mini-golf, there's something for everyone in this vibrant and eclectic area.

Bowling Alleys and More - A Strike of Fun in Eugene

Emerald Lanes - Located at 140 Oakway Rd, Eugene, OR 97401, Welcome to Emerald Lanes! This alley is known for its well-maintained lanes and lively atmosphere. Open since 1959 Emerald is the premier bowling center in our region. We specialize in fun, family, and the sport of bowling. We have 24 updated synthetic lanes and automatic bumpers for the kids. We have a full restaurant and a fully stocked pro shop.

Visit https://emeraldlaneseugene.com/ for details

Strike City Bowling Center - Strike City, situated at 1170 W 2nd Ave, Eugene, OR 97402, is a popular spot among locals. With its modern facilities and a welcoming ambiance, they are your one-stop shop for classic games, great food, and all-ages fun. Whether you're playing mini-golf or bowling with family, catching happy hour with friends, or watching the Ducks game, we've got you covered.

Visit https://www.entertainmenteugene.com/

Round1 USA is a multi-entertainment facility that brings an array of fun activities under one roof. They offer classic and modern entertainment options, including arcade games featuring a mix of new and retro games and bowling with state-of-the-art lanes.

Billiards and ping-pong are available for those who enjoy more traditional games. Karaoke rooms allow music enthusiasts to showcase their talents. Spo-Cha is a unique attraction for sports lovers, and there's also a dedicated kids' play zone for younger guests.

In addition, Round1 has a Victory Zone for special events and challenges, and to top it all off, they offer food and bar services to keep the fun going. This diverse range of activities makes Round1 an ideal spot for all ages and interests, whether it's for a family outing, a night out with friends, or a special event.

Visit at https://www.round1usa.com/

Emerald Valley USBC - At 1187 Fairfield Ave, Eugene, OR 97402, Emerald Valley USBC is a local favorite. This bowling center hosts tournaments and leagues, catering to those who take their bowling more seriously, yet it's also welcoming to casual players.

Visit at https://evusbc.com/

Today's bowling alleys are a far cry from the traditional venues of the past. They have transformed into vibrant entertainment centers that combine classic bowling fun with a plethora of modern amenities. These places now boast state-of-the-art lanes with digital scoring, mood lighting, and even themed nights. Alongside bowling, they offer diverse activities like arcade gaming, billiards, and karaoke, catering to a wide range of interests and ages. With gourmet food options and well-stocked bars, these alleys have become trendy spots for socializing and enjoying a night out. The shift towards offering a comprehensive entertainment experience makes them appealing to bowling enthusiasts and anyone looking for an enjoyable outing.

12

Hops, Barrels, and Cheers A Journey Through Eugene's Exceptional Craft Beer Scene

Ninkasi Brewing, located at 155 Blair Blvd, Eugene, OR 97402, stands out as a rapidly growing craft brewery in the United States. Famous for their top-selling IPA in Oregon, they also welcome visitors to their "Better Living Room" taproom, which offers ample indoor and outdoor seating. The taproom doubles as a restaurant and beer garden, celebrating beer, food, art, and community. Local ingredients flavor their delicious dishes, and IPA enthusiasts will find a haven here. Try their Tricerahops IPA and visit ninkasibrewing.com or call 541-735-9500 for more information.

Falling Sky Brewing, with locations including 1334 Oak Alley, Eugene, OR 97401, offers over 400 beer recipes since 2012. The brewpub, pour house, and pizzeria serve tasty eats and a variety of handcrafted brews. Notable beers include Dreadnut Foreign Export Stout and Daywalker Irish Red. Visit fallingskybrewing

.com or call 541-505-7096.

Alesong Brewing and Blending, at 80848 Territorial Hwy, Eugene, OR 97405, specializes in barrel-aged blends, reminiscent of old-world Lambic blenders and winemakers. Visit their countryside taproom for panoramic views and unique beers like Mocha Rhino Suit. Visit alesongbrewing.com or call 541-844-9925.

Hop Valley Brewing, located at 990 W 1st Ave, Eugene, OR 97402, is renowned for its creative brews. The tasting room offers a cozy environment with 25 beers on tap, including popular IPAs with cryo hops. Try their Citrus Mistress IPA. Visit hopvalleybrewing.com or call (541) 485-2337.

Oakshire Brewing, at 207 Madison St, Eugene, OR 97402, is dedicated to crafting exceptional beer. In the Whitaker neighborhood, they focus solely on brewing, with food trucks providing diverse culinary options. Sample their Watershed IPA and Overcast Espresso Stout. Visit oakbrew.com or call (541) 654-5520.

Claim 52 Brewing, at 1203 Willamette St #140, Eugene, OR 97401, excels in Northwest-style IPAs and innovative brews. They're known for hazy, tropical IPAs and fruit-infused beers. Fluffy Hazy IPA is a standout. Visit claim52brewing.com or call 458-205-8188.

Viking Braggot Brewing, at 2490 Willamette St, Eugene, OR 97405, is unique for its braggots - a mead-beer blend. Enjoy Scandinavian dishes with their Battle Axe IPA with Wildflower

Honey. Visit drinkviking.com or call 541-653-8371.

Coldfire Brewing Company, at 263 Mill St, Eugene, OR 97401, merges European brewing traditions with Northwestern flair. Their patio is perfect for sunny days, and their Cumulus Tropicalus Hazy IPA is a must-try. Visit coldfirebrewing.com or call 541-636-3889.

Gratitude Brewing, located at 540 E 8th Ave, Eugene, OR 97401, specializes in hoppy beers and kettle sours. Located in The Old Foundry building, it offers a range of traditional and unique beers, like Keep it Hazy Eugene. Visit gratitudebrewing.com or call 541-654-5009.

Another reason I love my community is the passion we have for doing something our way. These breweries often serve as gathering spots for locals and visitors, fostering a sense of camaraderie and community engagement. Each brewery's unique flavors and styles add to the local culture and economy, often supporting local events and charities. This thriving brewery scene offers a variety of artisan beers. It has become a hub for social interaction and cultural events and a testament to the region's creativity and entrepreneurial spirit.

13

Vineyards and Vintages Discovering the Enchanting Wineries of Eugene

King Estate Winery, a beacon of bio-dynamic winemaking since 1991, is the largest certified bio-dynamic vineyard in the US and a producer of award-winning wines. Their Pinot Gris and Pinot Noir are especially noteworthy. Visit them at 80854 Territorial Hwy, Eugene, OR 97405, and taste their exquisite collection, including the North by Northwest label wines. Visit them at https://kingestate.com. for more information and events.

Sarver Winery Nestled in scenic landscapes, family-owned Sarver Winery at 25600 Mayola Ln, Eugene, OR 97402, is known for its estate-grown, crisp white wines and earthy Pinots. Their cozy tasting room offers breathtaking views of the Valley and Three Sisters, complementing their delicious Pinot Noir, Pinot Gris, Riesling, Early Muscat, and Gewürztraminer. Visit them at https://www.sarverwinery.com.

Silvan Ridge Winery As Eugene's first bonded winery, Silvan Ridge, located at 27012 Briggs Hill Rd, Eugene, OR 97405, boasts a heritage dating back to 1979. Under the leadership of Juan Pablo "JP" Valot, they offer renowned wines like Pinot Noir, Pinot Gris, Malbec, and a Cabernet Sauvignon and Tempranillo blend, all enjoyed with stunning views. Visit them at https://sil vanridge.com.

Sweet Cheeks Winery, at 27007 Briggs Hill Rd, Eugene, OR 97405, offers wines as captivating as the hills surrounding its vineyard. Its tasting room, known for its relaxed atmosphere and stunning views, is a haven for tasting flights of Southern Willamette Valley's finest. Visit it at https://sweetcheekswiner y.com.

Iris Vineyards Explore the expansive 870-acre estate of Iris Vineyards at 82110 Territorial Hwy, Eugene, OR 97405. With a 43-acre vineyard growing Pinot Gris, Chardonnay, and Pinot Noir, they're a testament to the region's viticultural prowess. Visit them at https://sweetcheekswinery.com..

Oregon Wine LAB Urban and chic, Oregon Wine L.A.B. at 488 Lincoln St, Eugene, OR 97401 offers a modern twist on the traditional wine-tasting experience. This urban winery and bar features a selection of local and international wines, complemented by Eugene Weekly's Best Food Cart, Da Nang Vietnamese Eatery. Check their calendar for vibrant events at https://www. oregonwinelab.com.

Capitello Wines Blending Oregon's wine-making heritage with New Zealand roots, Capitello Wines presents artisanal wines in their tasting room at 540 Charnelton St, Eugene, OR 97401. Located in the historic former Lord Leebrick Theatre, they're open from Tuesday to Saturday, offering an array of reds, whites, and sparkling wine. Visit them at https://www.capitellowines.com.

Territorial Vineyards & Wine Company is located at 907 W 3rd Ave, Eugene, OR 97402 and they welcome you for a delightful tasting experience. Their portfolio includes Pinot Gris, Riesling, Chardonnay, Early Muscat, and an impressive selection of Pinot Noir. Visit them at https://territorialvineyards.com.

Eugene's winery scene is both vibrant and diverse, offering everything from cool urban tasting rooms to elegant vineyards. Each destination provides a unique glimpse into the world of wine-making, making Eugene a true paradise for wine enthusiasts.

14

Celebrating Eugene's Annual Events A Year-Round Festival Calendar

Mount Pisgah Wildflower and Music Festival - Every May, nature and music enthusiasts gather at Mount Pisgah for a celebration of natural beauty and melodious tunes. The festival is a vibrant mix of wildflower displays, live music, and outdoor enjoyment, perfect for families and nature lovers. Visit their website to find the dates https://mountpisgaharboretum.org/festivals-events/wildflower-music-festival.

Eugene Marathon, Every April—A highlight for runners, the Eugene Marathon transforms the city into a runner's paradise. From beginners to seasoned athletes, the event offers various races and a lively atmosphere, culminating in an unforgettable race experience. For all the details and information, visit eugenemarathon.com.

Eugene Pro Rodeo, July 4 - Celebrate Independence Day with a bang at the Eugene Pro Rodeo. Witness thrilling rodeo events, patriotic displays, and a community coming together in the spirit of America's cowboy heritage. Visit them at eugeneprorodeo.com

Butte to Butte, July 4 Held on the same day as the Eugene Pro Rodeo, Butte to Butte is a beloved local running event. Participants enjoy a scenic route, challenging themselves while experiencing Eugene's beautiful landscapes. Visit them at buttetobutte.com

Oregon Country Fair, Arriving mid-July—A magical experience awaits at the Oregon Country Fair. This festival is a blend of art, music, and culture, set in a whimsical outdoor environment. It's a celebration of creativity and community spirit. For exact dates and times, visit oregoncountryfair.org.

Asian Celebration, Late July - Immerse yourself in Asian culture at the annual Asian Celebration. This event features traditional performances, cuisine, and art, showcasing the rich diversity of Asian heritage. For exact dates and locations, visit asiancelebra tion.org.

Scandinavian Festival - Junction City, celebrated in August - Experience the charm of Scandinavia in Oregon. This festival in Junction City is a vibrant showcase of Scandinavian culture, complete with traditional foods, dances, and crafts. For times and dates of events, visit junctioncityscandia.org.

Hamadang Martial Arts Festival Held in early May - Witness the art and discipline of martial arts at the Hamadang Festival. This event brings together martial artists from various disciplines, offering demonstrations, workshops, and competitions. For dates and times, visit oshanmadang.com.

Bohemia Mining Days - Cottage Grove, July. Step back in time at the Bohemia Mining Days Festival in Cottage Grove. This event celebrates the region's mining history with a parade, historical reenactments, and fun family activities. Please visit bohemiami ningdays.org for dates and times.

Lane County Home & Garden Show, set for March at 796 W, 13th Ave., Eugene, OR 97402, is a premier event for home improvement and gardening enthusiasts. This show features a wide array of exhibits on the latest in home and garden trends, including landscaping, decor, and sustainable living solutions. Attendees can enjoy free seminars and demonstrations from industry experts, offering valuable tips and insights for home and garden projects. The show is renowned for its stunning garden displays, inspiring outdoor living spaces, and innovative landscaping ideas. Visitors can explore various home improvement solutions, meet with professionals, and take advantage of special show-only deals. Shopping opportunities abound, with a range of products from garden tools and plants to home appliances and decor. The event is designed to be family-friendly, making it an ideal outing for all ages. The Lane County Home & Garden Show is the perfect destination for those looking to enhance their living spaces, both indoors and out. Check out the website for all the events and dates https://eugenehomesh ow.com.

Eugene's calendar is packed with events that cater to a wide range of interests, from outdoor adventures and cultural celebrations to historical festivals and athletic challenges. Each event offers a unique way to experience the vibrant community spirit and diverse cultural heritage of Eugene and its surrounding areas.

15

Nature and Wildlife

Cascade Raptor Center: A Sanctuary for Birds of Prey

The Cascade Raptor Center, nestled in the lush landscapes of Eugene, Oregon, is a haven dedicated to the conservation and rehabilitation of birds of prey. This center plays a crucial role in educating the public about these magnificent birds and their importance to the ecosystem.

Discover the Majestic World of Raptors:

1. **Rehabilitation and Conservation** – The primary mission of the Cascade Raptor Center is the rehabilitation of injured or orphaned raptors. The center provides medical care, nurturing, and a safe space for recovery, with the ultimate goal of releasing healthy birds back into the wild.

2. **Educational Programs** - The center offers a range of educational programs aimed at all age groups. These programs provide valuable insights into the lives of raptors, their role in the environment, and the challenges they

face. Educational visits are an opportunity to learn about conservation efforts and how to coexist peacefully with these birds.

3. **Public Visitation and Bird Viewing** - Visitors to the center can view a variety of raptor species up close. The center houses eagles, hawks, falcons, owls, and other birds of prey, each with its own story. The enclosures are designed to mimic natural habitats, providing a respectful and safe viewing experience.

4. **Volunteer and Community Involvement** - The Cascade Raptor Center encourages community involvement through its volunteer programs. Volunteers play a vital role in caring for the birds, maintaining the facility, and assisting with educational programs.

Visitor Information:

- **Location:** 32275 Fox Hollow Rd, Eugene, OR 97405.
- **Contact:** For more information, to plan a visit, or to inquire about volunteer opportunities, call (541) 485-1320.
- **Website:** www.cascaderaptorcenter.org

Additional Services:

- **Adopt-a-Raptor Program** - The center offers an Adopt-a-Raptor program, where individuals can sponsor a resident bird. This program helps fund the care of the birds and the operations of the center.
- **Special Events and Workshops** - Cascade Raptor Center also hosts special events, workshops, and training sessions on raptor care and conservation.

The Cascade Raptor Center is more than a rehabilitation facility; it's a place where visitors can connect with nature and learn about the fascinating world of raptors. Whether you're an avid birdwatcher, a conservation enthusiast, or simply looking for a unique educational experience, the Cascade Raptor Center offers an opportunity to observe and appreciate these majestic birds in a beautiful, natural setting.

Delta Ponds is an amazing 150-acre natural area featuring a network of ponds, channels, wetlands, and riparian zones along the Willamette River. It's well known for bird watching, fishing, and outdoor enjoyment, such as strolling along the paths and reinvigorating yourself. The area has undergone significant restoration, reconnecting it with the river and improving habitats for species like juvenile Chinook salmon and Western pond turtles. A 1.5-mile loop trail offers easy access for exploration and appreciation of this diverse ecosystem. It's a great destination for those interested in nature, wildlife, and outdoor activities.

Between 2004 and 2012, the City of Eugene led a large-scale effort to restore the Delta Ponds as a side channel of the Willamette River. The goals that this project set out to achieve were to: (1) re-establish hydrological connections between the main stem Willamette River and the Delta Ponds to restore 2.2 miles of side-channel habitat to the Willamette River; (2) improve in-stream and riparian habitat for a wide variety of species including juvenile Chinook salmon, American beaver, western pond turtle, river otter, and Neo-tropical migratory birds; (3) improve water quality; and (4) provide recreational and educational opportunities to the public that would lead to increased stewardship of this valuable natural area.

Fish and wildlife monitoring efforts have shown the presence of juvenile Chinook salmon in the ponds during winter months, documented the use of the area by 155 species of birds, and identified a population of nearly 60 Western pond turtles.

For more details, you can visit their website at https://eugene-or.gov/Facilities/Facility/Details/Delta-Ponds-133

16

Day Trip Attractions Exploring the Wonders Around Eugene

Wildlife Safari: A Journey into the Wild, Just 80 miles South of Eugene

Embark on an exciting drive-through safari adventure at Wildlife Safari, situated in the picturesque landscape of Winston,

Oregon, approximately 60 miles south of Eugene. This unique wildlife park provides a one-of-a-kind opportunity to encounter exotic animals in a setting that closely resembles their natural habitats.

The Safari Experience:

1. **Drive-Through Adventure** - Wildlife Safari offers a thrilling 4.5-mile drive-through experience where you can view animals roaming freely in large enclosures. From the comfort of your vehicle, witness a variety of wildlife, including African lions, giraffes, cheetahs, elephants, and bears, in a more natural and expansive environment than traditional zoos.

2. **Up-Close Animal Encounters** - The park provides special encounters allowing guests to get closer to certain animals. These interactive experiences might include feeding a giraffe, meeting a cheetah, or observing elephants up close, providing a deeper understanding and appreciation of these magnificent creatures.

3. **Educational Programs** - Wildlife Safari is dedicated to conservation and education. It offers educational programs for all ages, including guided tours, keeper talks, and summer camps, making it a fantastic destination for families and school groups.

4. **Conservation Efforts** - The park plays a vital role in wildlife conservation, participating in global efforts to protect endangered species. By visiting, you contribute to these conservation initiatives, supporting the park's mission to preserve wildlife and educate the public.

5. **Village and Walking Areas** - In addition to the drive-through section, Wildlife Safari features a village area

where you can stroll and see more animals, such as cheetahs and flamingos. The village also includes dining options, a gift shop, and a children's petting zoo.

Visitor Information:

- **Location:** 1790 Safari Rd, Winston, OR 97496.
- **Contact:** For more information, tickets, and specific encounter bookings, visit <u>wildlifesafari.net</u> or call 541-679-6761.
- **Accessibility:** The park is accessible year-round, with different experiences available in each season.

Special Events and Activities:

- **Seasonal Events** - Wildlife Safari hosts various seasonal events throughout the year, such as holiday lights tours and Halloween celebrations.
- **Photography Opportunities** - The park is a haven for photographers, offering unique opportunities to capture wildlife in naturalistic settings.

Visiting Wildlife Safari is not just a fun day out; it's a journey into the world of wild animals and an opportunity to support vital conservation work. Whether you're a family looking for an educational adventure, a wildlife enthusiast, or a photographer in search of the perfect shot, Wildlife Safari offers an unforgettable experience that brings you face-to-face with nature's wonders, just a short drive from Eugene.

McKenzie River Trails is renowned for its beautiful waterfalls.

Some of the notable ones include Sahalie and Koosah Falls. Sahalie Falls is known for its powerful and picturesque cascade, while Koosah Falls offers a stunning display of water plunging into a deep pool. These waterfalls are among the highlights of the trail, providing scenic spots for photography and nature appreciation. For more details about these and other waterfalls along the McKenzie River Trail, you might want to look for resources that specifically detail the trail's features or visit https://oregonisforadventure.com/mckenzie-river-trail/

Lane County Covered Bridges has a notable collection of around 20 covered bridges, each with its unique design and history. Some of these include the Goodpasture Bridge, Lowell Bridge, Parvin Bridge, and the Office Bridge, among others. These bridges represent a range of architectural styles and historical eras, making them a fascinating subject for exploration. These historical bridges have survived fires, floods, and pestilence. They are a very important part of our history. For a complete list and detailed information about each bridge, you can visit the Eugene, Cascades & Coast website https://www.eugenecascadescoast.org/explore/history-culture-museums/covered-bridges/

The High Desert Museum in Bend is a comprehensive and interactive facility that offers insights into the high desert's natural history, wildlife, and cultural heritage. Here's an expanded look:

1. **Wildlife Exhibits:** Live animal exhibits featuring species native to the high desert, such as birds of prey and mam-

mals.

2. **Cultural Displays:** Artifacts and stories about the indigenous people of the region.

3. **Historical Exhibits:** Showcasing the pioneer and early settler era with reconstructed historical scenes.

4. **Art Exhibitions:** Featuring works related to or inspired by the high desert.

5. **Environmental Education:** Interactive displays explaining the unique geology and ecology of the area.

6. **Conservation Programs:** Highlighting efforts to protect local ecosystems and species.

7. **Interactive Kids' Zone:** Engaging activities designed for children to learn about nature and history.

8. **Guided Tours:** Educators provide in-depth information about the exhibits.

9. **Outdoor Trails:** Paths to explore the surrounding natural landscape.

10. **Special Events:** Workshops, lectures, and other educational programs.

For more detailed information about the museum's offerings and specific exhibits, please visit https://highdesertmuseum.org/.

Belknap Hot Springs, located along the scenic McKenzie River, offers a unique combination of natural beauty and relaxation. Here's a detailed summary:

1. **Location:** About an hour and 15 minutes from Eugene on Highway 126.

2. **Hot Springs Pools:** Fed by natural mineral hot springs, adjusted with McKenzie River water.
3. **Temperature Range:** Pools are maintained between 101 to 104 degrees Fahrenheit.
4. **Opening Hours:** Available from 9 a.m. to 9 p.m. year-round.
5. **Entry Fee:** Options include $8 per hour or $15 for the day, per person.
6. **Lush Gardens:** The resort features beautifully maintained gardens for a serene experience.
7. **Hiking Opportunities:** Surrounded by natural trails, ideal for exploring the Oregon wilderness.
8. **Relaxation and Rejuvenation:** The hot springs and natural setting offer a perfect retreat.
9. **Forest Setting:** Nestled in a forested area, providing a tranquil atmosphere.
10. **Accessibility:** Easy to access for both day visitors and overnight guests.

For more details, visit belknaphotsprings.com.

Sandland Adventures in Florence offers a variety of activities:

- **Giant Dune Buggy Tours:** A mix of scenic beauty and excitement across dunes and beach.
- **Miniature Golf:** An 18-hole course set among beautiful flowers and waterfalls.
- **Bumper Boats:** A fun water ride with motorized, steerable boats.

- **Cloverline Railroad:** A scenic rail tour through tunnels, woodlands, and gardens.
- **Go-Karts:** A 1/4 mile grandprix style track for driving excitement.

For more details on these adventures, visit HTTPS://www.sand land.com/

Dee Wright Observatory: A Stone Window to the Cascades

Embark on a magical journey to the Dee Wright Observatory, a stone sentinel in the Cascade Mountains. This extraordinary structure, crafted entirely from lava rock by the Civilian Conservation Corps in the 1930s, is a testament to natural beauty and human ingenuity.

A scenic 90-minute drive from Eugene transports you into a realm of awe-inspiring landscapes. Travel east on Highway 126, merging with Highway 20 near the Santiam Pass, and find yourself surrounded by nature's grandeur. Along the way, marvel at the towering sights of Mount Washington and Three Fingered Jack, the vibrant hues of red vine maples in autumn, and serene mountain lakes.

The observatory, reminiscent of an ancient castle, is perched at the summit amidst vast lava fields that stretch across the horizon. Here, you are granted an unobstructed, 360-degree panorama of the volcanic landscape, with six majestic Cascade peaks, including the Three Sisters, coming into full view.

Step outside to the interpretive trail, a path weaving through the intriguing lava beds, offering a unique walking experience. This trail provides insights into the region's volcanic history and allows you to witness the resilience of life as flora and fauna thrive amidst the lava rock.

The Dee Wright Observatory isn't just a destination; it's a journey through time and nature. This spot is a treasure waiting to be discovered for photographers, nature lovers, and anyone seeking a glimpse into the heart of Oregon's wilderness. You'll feel a profound connection to the earth and its ancient stories as you stand within the observatory's stone walls, gazing at the sprawling vistas. https://www.fs.usda.gov/visit/destination/ dee-wright-observatory

Hwy 138- Roseburg Waterfalls: A Cascading Adventure

Embark on a mesmerizing journey along Hwy 138 near Roseburg, where stunning waterfalls await to enchant you. Less traveled by the tourist crowds, this route is a hidden gem for waterfall enthusiasts and nature lovers alike.

As you meander along Hwy 138, the landscape unfolds into a lush tapestry of verdant forests and rolling hills, setting the stage for the waterfalls' dramatic reveals. Each waterfall along this route has unique charm and character, ranging from thunderous cascades to serene, trickling falls.

Key Waterfalls to Explore:

1. **Watson Falls** - Nestled in the Umpqua National Forest, Watson Falls is a breathtaking sight. Plummeting 272 feet, it's one of the tallest waterfalls in Oregon. A relatively short hike leads you to an awe-inspiring viewpoint where the falls drop in a misty, roaring cascade.

2. **Toketee Falls** - Further along the route, Toketee Falls is renowned for its picturesque beauty. The water here

gracefully plunges over basalt columns, creating a two-tiered fall totaling 120 feet. The hike to the viewpoint winds through ancient forests, adding to the destination's mystique.

3. **Clearwater Falls—As its name suggests, Clearwater Falls is a serene and gentle waterfall. The waters elegantly cascade over moss-covered rocks, creating a tranquil atmosphere** perfect for relaxation and reflection.

4. **Lemolo Falls** - A visit to Lemolo Falls is a must for the more adventurous. The falls drop dramatically over a cliff, creating a powerful, awe-inspiring sight. The hike to the falls is a bit more challenging but rewards stunning views and a sense of seclusion.

5. **Fall Creek Falls—**This multi-tiered waterfall offers a spectacular view as it cascades through dense greenery. The trail to Fall Creek Falls is an easy, family-friendly hike accessible for all ages and skill levels.

Other Attractions Along the Way:

- **Diamond Lake** - Close to some of these waterfalls, Diamond Lake offers scenic beauty and recreational activities like fishing, boating, and camping.
- **Umpqua Hot Springs—**For a relaxing end to your waterfall adventure, consider a visit to Umpqua Hot Springs, where natural thermal pools overlook the beautiful forested valley.

As you journey along Hwy 37 near Roseburg, each waterfall presents an opportunity to connect with nature in its purest form. Whether you are looking for an adventurous hike, a peaceful spot to unwind, or the perfect photo opportunity, this waterfall trail offers an unforgettable experience. So, pack your camera, lace up your hiking boots, and prepare to be captivated by the natural splendor of Roseburg's waterfalls. https://orego n.com/attractions/falls-north-umpqua-river

Crater Lake: A Deep Blue Wonder in Oregon's Backyard

Embark on a journey to Crater Lake, a natural marvel nestled in the heart of Oregon. As one of the state's most iconic landmarks, Crater Lake astonishes visitors with its deep, vivid blue waters and the sheer cliffs that encircle it. Formed over 7,000 years ago by the collapse of the volcano Mount Mazama, Crater Lake is the deepest lake in the United States and one of the most pristine on Earth.

Experiencing Crater Lake:

1. **Rim Drive**—This scenic drive around the lake offers breath-taking viewpoints and photo opportunities. The 33-mile Rim Drive encircles the lake, providing access to over 30 overlooks where you can stop and absorb the stunning vistas.
2. **Boat Tours—Consider taking a boat tour to examine the lake's majesty closely**. These guided tours offer an up-close perspective of the lake's crystal-clear waters and geological wonders, including the famous Phantom Ship, a natural rock formation.
3. **Hiking Trails** - Crater Lake National Park boasts a variety of trails for all skill levels. From easy walks along the rim to more strenuous hikes down to the water's edge, each trail offers unique views and experiences. The Cleetwood Cove Trail, the only legal access to the lake shore, is a must-do

for those wishing to touch the lake's waters or swim.

4. **Wizard Island** - A visit to Crater Lake isn't complete without seeing Wizard Island, a cinder cone rising from the lake's surface. Accessible by boat, the island offers hiking trails and spectacular views, especially from the summit.

5. **Stargazing** - Due to its high elevation and remote location, Crater Lake is an ideal spot for stargazing. On clear nights, the sky above the lake is filled with stars, planets, and constellations, creating a mesmerizing celestial display.

6. **Winter Wonderland** - In winter, Crater Lake transforms into a snowy paradise. Snowshoeing and cross-country skiing are popular activities, offering a different perspective of the lake's beauty amidst the tranquility of the snow-covered landscape.

7. **Visitor Information:Location:** Crater Lake National Park, in southwestern Oregon.

- **Accessibility:** The park is open year-round, but some roads and facilities are closed in winter due to snow.
- **Visitor Centers:** The Rim Village Visitor Center and the Steel Visitor Center offer exhibits, park information, and ranger-led programs.

-

For more information visit: Visit Crater Lake

Crater Lake Zipline: Soaring High Over Southern Oregon's Natural Beauty

The Crater Lake Zipline experience is a must-try for an adrenaline-filled adventure that complements the tranquil beauty of Crater Lake. It is one of the most exciting ways to witness the majestic landscapes of Southern Oregon and offers a unique perspective of the region's natural splendor.

The Zipline Experience:

1. **Klamath Basin Views**—The Crater Lake Zipline is located in the nearby Klamath Basin, not directly at Crater Lake. It offers a thrilling aerial view of the surrounding forests, mountains, and wildlife. As you zip through the sky, panoramic vistas of the Cascade Range unfold beneath you, providing a breathtaking backdrop.

2. **Longest Zipline in Oregon** - Boasting the title of the longest zipline in Oregon, this canopy tour includes nine ziplines, ranging in length, the longest being over a quarter-mile. Each line offers a different thrill and view, making the entire experience varied and exciting.

3. **Sky Bridges and Rappels**—Two sky bridges and two rappels add to the adventure. The sky bridges provide a moment to pause and soak in the surroundings from a unique vantage point, while the rappels offer an exhilarating descent back to the ground.

4. **Treetop Platforms** - The course's treetop platforms are strategically placed to maximize your views and excitement. They also provide a moment of rest and an opportunity to learn about the local ecology from knowledgeable guides.

5. **Sustainable Adventure** - The zipline is committed to sustainability and Eco-friendly practices, ensuring that the adventure is not only thrilling but also respectful of the natural environment.

6. **Guided Experience** - Each tour is guided by experienced and friendly staff, ensuring safety and providing insight

into the region's history, flora, and fauna.

7. **Visitor Information:**
8. **Location:** 29840 Highway 140 West, Klamath Falls, OR 97601.
9. **Website:** craterlakezipline.com
10. **Contact:** For bookings and inquiries, visit their website or call the Crater Lake Zipline team.

Additional Activities:

1. **Kayak and Canoe Tours** - For those looking to explore the waters, the zipline's sister company, ROE! Real Oregon Experience offers kayak and canoe tours in the surrounding waterways.
2. **Winter Adventures** - In the winter months, snowshoeing tours are available, offering a serene exploration of the snow-covered landscape.
3. The **Crater Lake Zipline** is more than just an adventure; it's an exhilarating journey through the heart of Oregon's natural beauty. It's an ideal addition for those visiting Crater Lake National Park or exploring the wider Klamath Basin area, providing a unique and unforgettable perspective of one of the most beautiful regions in the Pacific Northwest.

Visiting Crater Lake is more than just a day trip; it's an immersion into one of nature's most awe-inspiring creations. Whether seeking adventure, tranquility, or simply a stunning view, Crater Lake's deep blue waters and majestic surroundings promise an unforgettable experience.

C&M Stables - Horseback Riding: A Coastal Equestrian Adventure

C&M Stables, nestled along the stunning Oregon coastline in Florence, offers a unique and memorable way to experience the natural beauty of the Pacific Northwest. Located at 90241 Hwy 101 N, Florence, OR 97439, this stable provides an exceptional opportunity for novice and experienced riders to explore the breathtaking Oregon coast on horseback.

Experiencing Horseback Riding at C&M Stables:

1. **Guided Beach Rides** - One of the highlights of C&M Stables is their guided beach rides. These rides take you along the serene Oregon beaches, where the rhythmic sound of the waves and the vast expanse of the ocean create a tranquil backdrop. It's an ideal way to connect with nature and uniquely experience the coast.

2. **Variety of Riding Trails** - Besides beach rides, C&M Stables offers a variety of trails that wind through the picturesque coastal forest and dunes. These trails offer a different perspective of the region's diverse landscape, from dense woodland to open sandy expanses.

3. **Horses for All Skill Levels** - The stables cater to all levels of riding experience, from beginners to advanced riders. Their well-trained and gentle horses ensure a safe and enjoyable ride for everyone.

4. **Educational Aspect** - Experienced guides accompany all rides, providing safety and guidance and sharing knowledge about the local ecology, history, and horseback riding techniques.

5. **Unique Rides and Packages** - C&M Stables offers various

riding packages, including private, sunset, and special occasion packages such as proposals or anniversary celebrations.

Visitor Information:

- **Location:** 90241 Hwy 101 N, Florence, OR 97439.
- **Contact:** For inquiries, reservations, or more information, call 541.997.7540 or visit oregonhorsebackriding.com.
- **Hours and Bookings:** It's recommended to book in advance, especially during peak seasons, to ensure availability.

Amenities and Services:

- **Horse Riding Lessons** – C&M Stables offers lessons for all age groups and skill levels for those interested in learning more about horseback riding.
- **Event Hosting** – The stables can also host group events, including family gatherings, corporate retreats, and educational trips.

Riding with C&M Stables is more than just a horseback ride; it's an immersive experience that combines the thrill of equestrian adventure with the unparalleled beauty of the Oregon coast. Whether you're seeking a peaceful ride along the beach, a scenic journey through coastal forests, or a special way to celebrate an occasion, C&M Stables promises an unforgettable experience that connects you with nature and the majestic world of horses.

Ocean Breeze ATV Rentals: Conquer the Dunes of Florence

Prepare yourself for an exhilarating experience with Ocean Breeze ATV Rentals, a gateway to the adventurous world of ATV riding on the magnificent dunes of Florence, Oregon. This rental service allows thrill-seekers and nature enthusiasts alike to explore one of the most unique landscapes in the Pacific Northwest.

The ATV Riding Experience:

1. **Diverse Range of ATVs** - Ocean Breeze ATV Rentals boasts a fleet catering to all skill levels, from beginners to experienced riders. Whether you prefer a leisurely ride or an adrenaline-fueled adventure, an ATV awaits you.

2. **Scenic Dune Landscape—The Florence dunes offer** picturesque and thrilling terrain for ATV riding. Spanning miles along the coast, these dunes provide a variety of trails and areas to explore, from gentle slopes to challenging ridges.

3. **Family-Friendly Adventure** - ATV riding at Ocean Breeze is an activity for the whole family. With safety as a priority, they offer vehicles and guidance suitable for all ages, making it a perfect outing for everyone.

4. **Expert Guidance and Safety—For those new to ATV riding, Ocean Breeze provides expert instruction and safety briefings to ensure a secure and enjoyable experience. Their knowledgeable staff is** on hand to assist with all aspects of the adventure.

5. **Convenient Location and Accessibility** - Situated in the heart of Florence's dune country, Ocean Breeze ATV Rentals is easily accessible and an ideal starting point for your dune exploration.

Visitor Information:

- **Location:** Florence, Oregon.
- **Contact:** To book an ATV or for more information, call 541-321-8484, email OceanBreezeATVRental@gmail.com, or visit florenceoregonatvrentals.com.

Other Activities and Services:

- **Guided Tours** – For those who prefer a guided experience, Ocean Breeze offers ATV tours led by experienced guides who can take you to the best spots on the dunes.
- **Group and Event Bookings** – Ocean Breeze can accommodate groups for special occasions, corporate events, or group outings, providing a unique and memorable experience.

An adventure with Ocean Breeze ATV Rentals is not just about riding an ATV; it's about immersing yourself in the natural beauty of the Oregon coast and experiencing the thrill of navigating through one of nature's most fascinating playgrounds. Whether you're a seasoned rider or a first-timer, a day spent conquering the Florence dunes promises excitement, fun, and memories that will last a lifetime.

Sea Lion Caves: A Spectacular Marine Wildlife Encounter

Venture into the Sea Lion Caves at 91560 Hwy 101 N, Florence, OR 97439 for an unforgettable experience with nature's marine wonders. This unique wildlife preserve and bird sanctuary offers a rare opportunity to observe sea lions in a natural habitat, along with various seabirds and other marine life.

Discovering the Sea Lion Caves:

1. **Natural Wonder** - The Sea Lion Caves are one of the largest connected systems of sea caves and caverns in the United States. Formed over 25 million years ago, these caves provide a haven for a large colony of Steller sea lions.

2. **Sea Lion Habitat—Depending on the season, you can witness sea lions lounging inside the caverns or on the rocky ledges outside. The viewing areas inside the caves offer a protected vantage point to observe** these fascinating creatures in their natural environment.

3. **Bird Watching** - The area is a sanctuary for sea lions and a haven for various seabird species. The rugged cliffs around the caves are nesting grounds for birds such as puffins, cormorants, and gulls, making it an excellent bird-watching spot.

4. **Educational Experience** - The Sea Lion Caves provide an educational experience with interpretive displays and knowledgeable staff. Learn about the lifecycle and habits of the sea lions, the geological history of the caves, and the conservation efforts to protect these incredible animals.

5. **Spectacular Views—The site offers breathtaking views of the Oregon Coast, with its dramatic cliffs and the vast Pacific Ocean. It's an ideal spot for photography and to simply enjoy the area's stunning natural beauty**.

Visitor Information:

- **Location:** 91560 Hwy 101 N, Florence, OR 97439.
- **Contact:** For more details or to plan your visit, call 541.547.3111 or visit sealioncaves.com.

Additional Attractions:

- **Gift Shop and Cafe** — The Sea Lion Caves facility includes a gift shop where you can purchase souvenirs and a café where you can relax and enjoy refreshments with an ocean view.
- **Whale Watching** - The location is also a prime spot for whale watching, especially during migration seasons. Visitors may glimpse gray whales as they travel along the Oregon coast.

Visiting the Sea Lion Caves is not just an outing; it's an immersion into a world where wildlife and nature coexist spectacularly. It's a place where you can connect with the raw power of the Pacific and the creatures that call it home. Whether you're a nature enthusiast, a family looking for an educational adventure, or a traveler seeking the unique beauty of the Oregon coast, the Sea Lion Caves are a must-visit destination.

Old-Growth Tree Climbing at Silver Falls State Park: A Canopy Adventure

Discover the exhilarating world of old-growth tree climbing at Silver Falls State Park, nestled in the verdant landscape of Sublimity, Oregon. This unique and immersive experience, offered by Tree Climbing at Silver Falls, takes adventure and nature connection to new heights, quite literally.

Climbing Amongst the Giants:

1. **Guided Climbing Tours** - The tree climbing adventures are guided by experienced instructors who ensure safety while teaching you the ropes, quite literally, of tree climbing.

This hands-on experience is educational and thrilling, suitable for beginners and seasoned climbers alike.

2. **Old-Growth Forest Setting** - The park's old-growth forest provides a majestic and serene backdrop for the climbing adventure. These towering trees, some of which have stood for centuries, offer a unique perspective on the natural world and an unparalleled connection with nature.

3. **Ecological Insights** - As you ascend the trees, guides provide fascinating information about the forest ecosystem, the biology of the trees, and the importance of conservation. It's an experience that educates as much as it exhilarates.

4. **All Ages Welcome** - Tree climbing at Silver Falls State Park is an activity that people of all ages can enjoy. It's a wonderful way for families to bond and for individuals to challenge themselves while immersed in nature.

5. **Safety and Equipment** - The highest safety standards are maintained, with top-quality climbing gear and safety harnesses provided. Participants are given a thorough briefing and constant guidance, ensuring a safe and enjoyable experience.

Visitor Information:

- **Location:** Silver Falls State Park, Sublimity, Oregon.
- **Contact:** For reservations and more information, call 206-914-8613 or email info@TreeClimbingAtSilverFalls.com. or visit https://www.treeclimbingatsilverfalls.com/

Additional Activities and Features:

- **Hiking and Waterfall Views** - Beyond tree climbing, Silver Falls State Park is renowned for its stunning waterfalls and extensive hiking trails. The park's famous Trail of Ten Falls is a hiker's paradise, offering scenic views of cascading waterfalls.
- **Photography Opportunities** - The unique vantage points from the treetops provide incredible photography opportunities, capturing the beauty of the forest canopy and the landscape below.

Old-Growth Tree Climbing at Silver Falls State Park is more than just an outdoor activity; it's an opportunity to connect with nature profoundly and excitingly. Whether you're looking for a new adventure, a family outing, or simply a peaceful retreat in the embrace of ancient trees, this experience promises to leave you with lasting memories and a deeper appreciation for the natural world.

These day trip attractions around Eugene offer diverse experiences, from the tranquility of natural hot springs and the excitement of dune buggies to the awe-inspiring beauty of Crater Lake and the unique experience of tree climbing. Each destination allows one to explore and appreciate Oregon's natural beauty and adventurous spirit.

17

Conclusion

In conclusion, this guidebook reflects my deep affection for Eugene Springfield, a place I've called home for nearly 25 years. From the moment I arrived, I was captivated by its vibrant energy, passionate community, and myriad of activities and sights. This region is truly a slice of heaven on Earth, with its unique blend of nature, culture, and community spirit. I hope this guide inspires both newcomers and locals alike to explore and support our local businesses, contributing to the vibrant tapestry that makes this state extraordinary. Enjoy discovering the wonders of Eugene Springfield!

Make a Difference with Your Review

Again, thank you so much for taking the time to read this book.

If you enjoyed it, please write a review. That is the best way for more people to appreciate all the wonders of Eugene-Springfield and the surrounding areas.

My big goal is to make the wonders of visiting Eugene-Springfield something anyone can experience. Everything I do is all about hitting that goal. And the only way to make that dream a reality is to spread the word to everyone.

And here's where you come in! Many people judge a book by its cover—or its reviews, to be exact. So, I'm asking for a little favor on behalf of a fellow explorer you haven't met yet.

Please leave a review for this book.

Your review might help...

...another small business thrives in its community.

...an entrepreneur supports their family with pride.

...someone lands a job that fills their life with purpose.

...a client finds that life-changing spark.

...make someone's dream a reality.

And all it takes to spread that joy is a quick review. Ready to feel awesome and make a real difference? Just scan the QR code below to leave your review:

QR Code for review page

If the thought of helping out a fellow Eugene-Springfield enthusiast brings a smile, you're my kind of person. Welcome to the club; you're one of the good ones.

I can't wait to share more about how you can dive deeper into the heart of Eugene-Springfield, discovering secrets and strategies that will make your journey even more magical. You're gonna love what's in store.

A huge thank you from the very bottom of my heart. Now, let's jump back into our adventure.

· Your biggest fan, Helen Williams

P.S. – Did you know? When you share something valuable, you become even more valuable to others. If this guide can help another explorer like you, why not spread the love and send this book their way?

18

References

Amtrak. (n.d.). https://amtrak.com/

Route schedules and maps > Lane Transit District. (n.d.). https://www.ltd.org/route-schedules-maps/

Pedego Eugene - Local Electric bike shop | Pedego Electric Bikes. (2024, January 21). Pedego Electric Bikes. https://pedego electricbikes.com/dealers/eugene/

Bike Share | Eugene, OR website. (n.d.). https://www.eugene-or.gov/3851/Bike-Share

Eugene — superpedestrian. (n.d.). Superpedestrian. https://s uperpedestrian.com/eugene

Aragon Alpacas in Eugene, Oregon>. (n.d.). http://aragonalpa cas.com/

Eugene, OR. (2023, October 6). Get Air Eugene | Best indoor trampoline park for family fun. https://getairsports.com/eugen e/

Hideaway Bakery. (n.d.). Hideaway Bakery. https://hideaway bakery.com/

Black Wolf Supper Club. (n.d.). https://www.blackwolfsupper

club.com/

Krob Krua | Wood Fired Thai. (n.d.). https://www.krobkrua.com/

Places to eat in Eugene | Restaurant Brewery | Steelhead Brewing Co. (2024, January 19). Steelhead Brewing Company. https://steelheadbrewery.com/brewery-restaurant-eugene/

Glendi Cafe – Eugene's Finest Meditteranean Food since 1999. (n.d.). https://glendicafe.com/

Best trails in Eugene. (n.d.). AllTrails.com. https://www.alltrails.com/us/oregon/eugene

River Trail Guides. (n.d.). Evan Wills - River Trail Guides. Evan Wills - River Trail Guides. https://www.rivertrailguides.com/

Eugene Canoe / Kayak / SUP Rentals! -. (2023, October 5). https://canoetour.org/

Cascade Adventure Company. (2023, June 22). Cascade Adventure Company. Cascade Adventure Company - Adventure Starts Here. https://www.cascadeadventureoregon.com/

Spencer Outfitters & Guides. (n.d.). Welcome to McKenzie River Fishing Guides & rafting Tours. Welcome to McKenzie River Fishing Guides & Rafting Tours. https://www.spenceroutfitters.com/

Oregon Rafting Adventures with Oregon Whitewater Adventures. (n.d.). http://www.oregonwhitewater.com/

Home Waters Fly Fishing – (541) 342-6691. (2023, June 16). Home Waters Fly Fishing. https://www.homewatersflyfishing.com/

Oregon guided fly fishing trips | The Caddis Fly: Oregon Fly Fishing blog. (n.d.). https://oregonflyfishingblog.com/guided-trips.

20x21 Mural Project | Eugene, OR website. (n.d.). https://www.eugene-or.gov/3492/20x21-Mural-Project

Homepage | Jordan Schnitzer Museum of Art. (n.d.). https://jsma.uoregon.edu/

Oregon Air and Space Museum. (n.d.). Oregon AIr and Space Museum. http://www.oasmuseum.com/

Planetarium. (n.d.). Eugene Science Center. https://eugenesciencecenter.org/planetarium/

Visit the museum | Museum of Natural and Cultural History. (n.d.). https://mnch.uoregon.edu/visit

Home – Adventure! Children's Museum. (2024, January 18). Adventure! Children's Museum. https://adventurechildrensmuseum.org./

Home | EmeraldArtCenter. (n.d.). EmeraldArtCenter. https://emeraldartcenter.org./

Hayward Field | University of Oregon. (n.d.). https://hayward.uoregon.edu/

Matthew Knight Arena - Concerts & Shows. (n.d.). https://goducks.com/feature/mka

Aragon Alpacas in Eugene, Oregon>. (n.d.). http://aragonalpacas.com/

Eugene, OR. (2023b, October 6). Get Air Eugene | Best indoor trampoline park for family fun. https://getairsports.com/eugene/

SMJ House | The Castle on the Hill. (2001, January 22). https://smjhouse.org/

Where Minds Grow: Using your library: museum. (n.d.). https://wheremindsgrow.org/your_library/museum

Symphony, E. (2023, May 12). Welcome to Eugene Symphony. Eugene Symphony. https://eugenesymphony.org/

Studio west. (n.d.). Studio west. Studio West. https://visitstudiowest.com/

Tsunami books. (n.d.). Tsunami Books. https://www.tsunami

books.org/

Hult Center for the Performing Arts. (n.d.). Hult Center for the Performing Arts. https://hultcenter.org/

Henry. (2024, January 19). WOW Hall homepage - WOW Hall. WOW Hall in Eugene Oregon. https://wowhall.org/

Home. (2024, January 3). Very Little Theatre. https://thevlt.com/

Richard E. Wildish Community Theater, Springfield, Oregon – Not a bad seat in the house. (n.d.). https://www.wildishtheater. com/

Actors Cabaret of Eugene | Live Musical Theatre | Eugene, OR, USA. (n.d.). Actorscabaret. https://www.actorscabaret.org/

V5, M. (n.d.). Oregon Contemporary Theatre. Oregon Contemporary Theatre. https://www.octheatre.org/

elleeyedesign. (2024, January 19). Home - the McDonald Theatre. The McDonald Theatre. https://mcdonaldtheatre.com/

University Theatre | Eugene's source for classic and experimental stage performances of high caliber at affordable prices. (n.d.). https://blogs.uoregon.edu/theatre/

Corporate, The Shedd Institute. (n.d.). The John G. Shedd Institute for the Arts. https://theshedd.org/

Lanearts. (n.d.). First Friday ArtWalk. Lane Arts Council. https://lanearts.org/first-friday-artwalk/

2nd Friday Art Walk | EmeraldArtCenter. (n.d.). EmeraldArtCenter. https://www.emeraldartcenter.org/second-friday

Vino and Vango. (2023, December 30). Home - Vino and vango. https://vinoandvango.com/

Oregon Axe throwing. (n.d.). Oregon Axe Throwing. https://www.oregonaxethrowing.com/

Portal Adventures - Immersive escape rooms in Oregon | Beaverton | Eugene | Springfield. (n.d.). Portal Adventures - Beaverton and Eugene. https://portaladventures.com/

Trapdoor puzzle and escape rooms. (n.d.). Trapdoor Puzzle and Escape Rooms. https://trapdooreugene.com./

Mental Mansion Escape Rooms | Escape the Room | Eugene Oregon. (n.d.). Mysite. https://www.mentalmansion.com/

Camp Putt | Willamalane Park and Recreation District. (n.d.). https://www.willamalane.org/facilities/camp_putt/index.php

Mike Gray - MG COMPUTER GROUP. (n.d.). The most fun you can have in Virtual Reality! https://multivrse.games/

Eugene Eats Food Tours LLC | food tours in Eugene | Oregon. (n.d.). EugeneEatsFoodTours. https://eugenefoodtours.com/

Paint & Sip & Local Art in Eugene OR. (n.d.). ART WITH ALEJANDRO. https://www.artwithalejandro.com/

Potters Quarter | Paint your own pottery | 2848 Willamette Street, Eugene, OR, USA. (n.d.). My Site. https://www.pottersquarter.com/

Onsen Hot Tub and Sauna Rentals | Eugene Oregon. (n.d.). https://www.onsenspas.com/

Eugene, OR. (2023c, October 6). Get Air Eugene | Best indoor trampoline park for family fun. https://getairsports.com/eugene/

Willamalane Park Swim Center | Willamalane Park and Recreation District. (n.d.). https://www.willamalane.org/facilities/willamalane_park_swim_center/index.php

Splash! at Lively Park | Willamalane Park and Recreation District. (n.d.). https://www.willamalane.org/facilities/splash!_at_lively_park/index.php

River Road Park and Recreation District is located in Eugene, Oregon. (n.d.). https://www.rrpark.org/

Amazon Pool | Eugene, OR website. (n.d.). https://eugene-or.gov/3223/Amazon-Pool

Emerald Lanes Bowling Center, Eugene, Oregon. (n.d.).

https://emeraldlaneseugene.com/

Entertainment Eugene. (n.d.). Entertainment Eugene. https://www.entertainmenteugene.com/

Round1 USA | All the fun under 1 roof. (n.d.). Round1 USA. https://www.round1usa.com/

Usbc, E. V. (n.d.). Emerald Valley USBC. Emerald Valley USBC. https://evusbc.com/

Ninkasi Brewing. (n.d.). Ninkasi Brewing | craft beer, cocktails, and restaurant in Eugene, OR. Ninkasi Brewing Company. https://ninkasibrewing.com/

Steelhead Brewing Company | Brewery restaurant in Eugene, Oregon. (2024, January 19). Steelhead Brewing Company. https://steelheadbrewery.com/

The Brewery | Falling Sky Brewing | Eugene, Oregon | Local Craft Beer. (n.d.). Falling Sky. https://fallingskybrewing.com/

Alesong Brewing & Blending. (n.d.). Alesong Brewing & Blending. https://alesongbrewing.com/

Home | Hop Valley Brewing. (n.d.). https://hopvalleybrewing.com/

Small batch brewing - Oakshire Brewing. (2024, January 1). Oakshire Brewing. https://oakbrew.com/

Claim 52 Brewing | Eugene Craft Brewery & Restaurant. (n.d.). Claim 52 Brewing. https://claim52brewing.com/

South Eugene Restaurant & Westside Brewery Taproom | Viking Brewing Co. (n.d.). Viking Brewing Co. https://drinkviking.com/

ColdFire Brewing. (n.d.). ColdFire Brewing. https://coldfirebrewing.com/

Elk Horn Brewery. (n.d.). https://elkhornbrewery.com/

Gratitude Brewing. (2024, January 21). Home - Gratitude Brewing. https://gratitudebrewing.com/

King Estate Winery Vineyard in Willamette Valley, Eugene, OR. (2022, April 18). King Estate Winery. https://kingestate.com/

Estate Grown Grapes | Sarver Winery | Oregon. (n.d.). Sarver-winery. https://www.sarverwinery.com/

Admin. (2024, January 10). Silvan Ridge - Heart of Oregon wine. Heart of Oregon Wine. https://silvanridge.com/

Sweet Cheeks Winery. (2022, November 28). Best wine tasting in Eugene, Oregon | Sweet Cheeks Winery. https://sweetcheeks winery.com/

Home - Iris Vineyards. (2023, March 9). Iris Vineyards. https://irisvineyards.com/

Oregon Wine L.A.B. (2023, June 20). Oregon Winery - Urban Winery - Eugene Winery | Oregon Wine LAB. https://www.oreg onwinelab.com/

Capitellowines. (2020, March 17). Capitello Wines - Capitello Wines. Capitello Wines. https://www.capitellowines.com/

Territorial Vineyards & Wine Company. (2022, February 3). Territorial Vineyards and Wine Company. Territorial Vineyards. https://territorialvineyards.com/

Wildflower & Music Festival – Mount Pisgah Arboretum. (n.d.). https://mountpisgaharboretum.org/festivals-events/ wildflower-music-festival/

Eugene Marathon. (n.d.). Eugene Marathon. https://eugene marathon.com/

Eugene pro Rodeo. (n.d.). Eugene Pro Rodeo. https://eugenep rorodeo.com/

Butte, B. T. (n.d.). Butte to butte. Butte to Butte. https://butte tobutte.com/

Oregon Country Fair. (n.d.). Oregon Country Fair. https://ore goncountryfair.org/

Oregon Asian Celebration. (n.d.). Oregon Asian Celebration.

https://asiancelebration.org/

Junction City Scandinavian Festival. (2024, January 2). Home - Scandinavian Festival & Culture of Junction City, Oregon. Scandinavian Festival & Culture of Junction City, Oregon. https://junctioncityscandia.org./

tgroup. (2024, January 19). Oregon State Hanmadang 2024. Oregon State Hanmadang. https://oshanmadang.com/

Bohemia Mining Days in Cottage Grove, Oregon – a festival for the entire family! (n.d.). https://bohemiaminingdays.org/

Welcome to Eugene Home Show. (2022, July 26). Eugene Home Show. https://eugenehomeshow.com/

Cascades Raptor Center. (n.d.). Cascades Raptor Center | Nature Center & Wildlife Hospital. https://cascadesraptorcenter.org/

Wildlife Safari. (n.d.). Wildlife Safari. https://wildlifesafari.net/

Delta ponds. (n.d.). Eugene, OR. https://eugene-or.gov/Facilities/Facility/Details/Delta-Ponds-133

Ragusa, N. (2021, August 21). Your guide to hiking the McKenzie River Trail. Oregon Is for Adventure. https://oregonisforadventure.com/mckenzie-river-trail/

Tour Twenty covered bridges across the Eugene, Cascades & Coast region. (n.d.). https://www.eugenecascadescoast.org/explore/history-culture-museums/covered-bridges/

High Desert Museum | Things to do in Bend Oregon. (2024, January 22). High Desert Museum. https://highdesertmuseum.org/

Belknap Hot Springs – McKenzie Bridge, Oregon. (n.d.). https://www.belknaphotsprings.com/

Sandland Adventures | Florence, Oregon | More than the Oregon Dunes. (n.d.). https://www.sandland.com/

Dee Wright Observatory | US Forest Service. (n.d.). US Forest Service. https://www.fs.usda.gov/visit/destination/dee-wright-observatory

Falls of the North Umpqua River. (n.d.). Oregon.com. https://oregon.com/attractions/falls-north-umpqua-river

Travel Oregon. (2023, December 27). Crater Lake National Park | Deep water in a sleeping volcano. https://traveloregon.com/things-to-do/destinations/lakes-reservoirs/crater-lake/?utm_actcampaign=967294047&gad_source=1

Crater Lake Zipline. (n.d.). https://craterlakezipline.com/

Turell Group. (2023, September 27). Horseback riding on the beach in Florence near Portland OR | C&M Stables. C&M Stables. https://oregonhorsebackriding.com/

Rentals, O. B. A. (n.d.). Ocean Breeze ATV Rentals. https://www.florenceoregonatvrentals.com/

Sea Lion Caves. (n.d.). Sea Lion Caves - America's largest sea cave - Florence, OR. https://www.sealioncaves.com/

Tree climbing and camping at Silver Falls State Park. (n.d.). Tree Climbing Silver. https://www.treeclimbingatsilverfalls.com/